New Directions in Theology Today

VOLUME V
Christian Life

New Directions in Theology Today
WILLIAM HORDERN, GENERAL EDITOR

VOL. I INTRODUCTION
BY WILLIAM HORDERN

VOL. II HISTORY AND HERMENEUTICS
BY CARL E. BRAATEN

VOL. III GOD
BY JOHN MACQUARRIE

VOL. IV THE CHURCH
BY COLIN WILLIAMS

VOL. V CHRISTIAN LIFE
BY PAUL HESSERT

VOL. VI MAN
BY ROGER L. SHINN

VOL. VII CHRIST
BY ROBERT CLYDE JOHNSON

NEW DIRECTIONS IN THEOLOGY TODAY

Volume V
Christian Life

BY
PAUL HESSERT

The Westminster Press
Philadelphia

LIBRARY OF CONGRESS CATALOG CARD NO. 67–12283

Published by The Westminster Press ®
Philadelphia, Pennsylvania

PRINTED IN THE UNITED STATES OF AMERICA

TO
ALTA MAE

Editor's Foreword

Theology always has existed in some tension with the church. But there is considerable evidence that today the gulf is wider than ever before. To both pastors and laymen it often seems that contemporary theology is working in opposition to the concerns of the parish. They are disturbed to read in newspapers and popular journals about theologians who seem to have lightly cast aside the cornerstones of the faith and who argue that the parish is doomed. To the theologian the parish often appears to be a respectable club dedicated to erecting buildings, raising budgets, and avoiding controversial issues.

There is little active dialogue between the theologian and the church today. The fault for this lies with both parties, but the situation is becoming increasingly serious as the church moves into a new age. This series is dedicated to the task of bridging the present gulf.

One of the reasons for the gulf between theology and the church is that neither the busy pastor nor the concerned layman can keep up to date with an ever-expanding theological literature. Thus, the purpose of New Directions in Theology Today is to present concise summaries of the present scene in theology. The series is not for the lazy pastor, nor for the layman who is beginning his theological education. Rather, these volumes are especially prepared for the busy pastor who is concerned with keeping abreast of modern theology and for the layman who, having been initiated into theology, is reading for further study, particularly to find out what contemporary Christian thinkers are saying.

The series is not written with the assumption that only professional theologians have something to say, but is offered in the hope that it will stimulate pastors and laymen to enter into the theological dialogue, and with the conviction that a vital theology for our time must be the work of the church as a whole.

WILLIAM HORDERN

Contents

Preface

In periods of theological uncertainty, a description of the Christian life may be the only way to restore order and perspective. Prior to the creation of theological systems, Christianity can only be described as a life. And when the intellectual framework of an age is called into question, that may be the form theology must again take.

Augustine wrote his handbook (*Enchiridion*) for Laurentius as an exposition of faith, hope, and love, although the section on faith overshadows the other two. The works of the Reformers are replete with descriptions of what is referred to today as the "style of life." William Ames, the Puritan theologian, held that theology comes out of life as shaped by Scripture, not out of Scripture as shaped by logic. John Wesley wrote that Christianity as a system of doctrine describes the character of a Christian, promises its realization, and tells how it is to be attained. The theological leaders of our age—Barth, Brunner, the Niebuhrs, and Bonhoeffer—have put their thought in the form of ethics.

What is the content of a discussion of the Christian life? There are the characteristics of the Christian himself in relation to his fellowmen—the love, joy, peace, patience, kindness, goodness, faithfulness, gentleness, and self-control which Paul cited as the fruits of the Spirit. Then there are the patterns of the Christian's relationship to the world. Is it a trap set by the evil one to snare him in his journey to the heavenly city? Is it a battleground to be approached with cunning? Is it the wilderness to be claimed and formed into Christ's realm from its neutral virgin innocence? Or is it already God's in such a way that the deluded who still carry on the fight—a noisy but vanquished minority—are to be neither feared nor attacked in anything like an all-out war of the Spirit? Finally, there is the life of the Christian community, the church, in which both personal and social aims are formulated and realized.

Some ages have had a fairly clear picture of the Christian, but ours is not one of them. We cannot make up our minds whether he takes his place within society as a substantial citizen or whether he must protest against the fundamental structures of that society. In some respects we want him to be conservative; in others we think he must be a revolutionary. We want him to assume responsibility and we want him to respect the rebel and beatnik. We want him to remain loyal to the organized church, reforming it from within, but we want him to be subtly aware of its irrelevancies. We are not clear about the voices that speak to him, whether they are of angels or devils.

The job of describing anything so comprehensive is immense and regardless of how carefully it is done there will still be serious omissions. "You haven't mentioned . . ." will be a common complaint whose fairness I already acknowledge. This book is part of a series and for that reason does not repeat the detailed examination of specific subjects to be found in the other volumes. On the other hand, major theological problems cannot be treated in isolation from the Christian life nor it in isolation from them. What I intend is not a catalog of views which remain distinct schemes of thought but a dialectical treatment of problems and relationships where acknowledged opposites nevertheless influence each other and where reporting and questioning proceed together. This results in a blending of sources which will irritate those who prefer their theology in separate blocks of pristine purity but it is much more honest to the way our minds do theology.

I should like to thank Dr. William Hordern, editor of the series, who first suggested the book but who is not to be charged for its shortcomings; my students—in particular Gary Vencill and Dennis Groh—whose pointed comments and questions helped focus the argument; and my family, who patiently put up with the invasion of their claims to my time and attention.

P. H.

Evanston, Illinois

CHAPTER I

Christian Life as Sanctification

A discussion of the Christian life is certainly unavoidable in considering the Christian faith, and yet the details of its description, including its definition, ground, power, and manifestation, are not easy to list or explain. Every Christian has an image in his mind of what the Christian life is, an ideal that both disturbs and inspires him, but an ideal that resists explicit description. Further, every Christian has something much more than an ideal: he has the reality of a new life in Christ, although frequently he does not see all the practical consequences of it. When equally committed Christians give almost diametrically opposite interpretations of the role of the Christian in today's world, there is not only the descriptive task of outlining these various views but the uniquely theological task of relating them to the gospel itself.

THE MEANING OF SANCTIFICATION

That somehow the Christian life is to be distinguished from the life of the human community in general is taken for granted in the New Testament. Jesus himself speaks of a righteousness beyond that even of the Pharisees which should characterize the disciple. (Matt. 5:20.) Paul frequently refers to the different standards that must prevail in the Christian community (e.g., I Cor. 6:1–8). The writer of the epistle to the Ephesians distinguishes Christians from "the nations" who are darkened in the futility of their minds, living in indifference and careless levity which the Christian must shun (Eph. 4:17–24). The immediate root of these admonitions is, no doubt, the church's heritage from Israel, the people called by God to be his witnesses in the world, a holy people. The church, too, saw itself as a holy priesthood, a peculiar people (I Peter 2:9–10). But at the same time, the setting aside of the Jewish cultus by the church[1] indicated that the manifestation of uniqueness would take other forms. The Didache might try to spell out the difference in terms of the particular days on which Christians fasted (Didache 8:1), and there is no question but that the controversy over the Sabbath as against the Lord's Day was meant to draw lines between Jews and Christians that all the world could see and appreciate. But the continuing problem of the church has been to probe behind such obvious distinctions to their ground in order that the true distinction might be something other than the superficial difference of fast days.

The distinction, if there is a valid one, must stem from the gospel itself. The focus of considerable theological probing today is on delineating authentic evangelical forms by which inherited customs can be evaluated and corrected. Otherwise, such changes as are made are simply the result of changing cultural forms and have no deeper rationale than the "spirit of the times." As usual in any such reappraisal, there have been persons who have simply denied the authority of inherited standards, thereby launching disturbing polemic along with real searching. Because of the rapid and radical changes within the culture at large, the current theological problem may be more intense than it has been for generations.

In relation to the gospel itself, however, the fundamental problem throughout the history of the church has been to avoid a Scylla and Charybdis in its doctrine of sanctification. Traditional theology has distinguished between justification as that which God does *for* men and sanctification as that which God does *in* men. The first has been called a relative change involving the relation to God, and the latter a real change involving a specific alteration in the life of the Christian. The danger lies in regarding the changed life as the *basis* of salvation, on the one hand, or as the expression of gratitude for the *act* of salvation, on the other—both of which turn the whole matter into an individual affair.

The New Testament itself faces this problem as it confronts legalisms of both sorts—i.e., those which seek self-justification before God (Rom. 3:27–28), and those which flow out from the new Christian orientation—"Do not taste, Do not touch" (Col. 2:21). Unfortunately the problem was not settled in that period even though the New Testament does give lines along which the issues must be drawn. God's act is not complete in a declaration, but only in the manifestation of the sons of God (Rom. 8:19–25); the good heart is productive of good deeds (Matt. 7:17–18).

Paul draws a distinction between the "outer man" which is wasting away and the "inner man" which is being renewed day by day (II Cor. 4:16). In this way the distinction between success in the life of this world and success in the life of the inner man is portrayed. The gifts of God's Spirit—love, joy, peace, patience, kindness, goodness, faithfulness, gentleness, self-control (Gal. 5:22)—are appropriate to the Christian regardless of his status in life, whether he is slave or master (I Cor. 7:17–24).

SANCTIFICATION AS RELEVANT DEVOTION

In the theology of the Middle Ages, this came to be spoken of as man's *supernatural* end as opposed to his *natural* end. His natural end was to develop and prosper as a natural organism with unique capacities within a social order. His supernatural end was to see God and to delight in that beatific vision. His Christian life, his sanctification, was to prepare him for his supernatural end, for only the pure in heart see God (Matt. 5:8). Almsgiving in its widest dimension of charitable works was done so that he might have mercy on his own soul. Because his natural equipment was sufficient only for his natural end, he needed the supernatural assistance of the church with its Sacraments to achieve his supernatural end.

This concern with the question as to how man finds salvation in the context of the two orders of reality, natural and supernatural, dominates the theology of the Middle Ages and sets the stage for the doctrinal work of the Reformers. A comparison of Reformation confessions with the dogmatic formulations of Nicaea and Chalcedon shows the movement of the intervening centuries. From the problem of the relation of the divine and human essences in Christ, attention shifts to the relation of divine grace and human will in the individual believer. In the concern for taking seriously the personal appropriation of Christ's salvation, nominalistic theology made grace function almost entirely within the structures of human self-determination. A rudimentary love of God, it held, was man's own possibility, which if exercised was rewarded with grace, making further acts of righteousness possible. The goal was Christlikeness which could merit eternal life.

This concern with the individual will had other theological repercussions. God himself was understood in terms of his will. This destroyed the possibility of grounding sacred doctrine in the order of things as science and philosophy can understand them, for between the world order and God lay his will—the ultimate locus of irrationality. With no "order of things" to fall back on, belief rested solely on human decision and thus belief itself became meritorious. And the acts of charity upon which salvation rested could no longer be defined simply in terms of human utility but only in terms of what God had arbitrarily declared would please him. The focus of charity, then, was not neighbor but God. Just those acts which had no human justification at all—pilgrimages, vigils, austerities, monastic endowments, and the like—became the proper service of God.

Agitation for church reform up to the events of 1517 protested the fundamental irrelevance so far as this world was concerned of such understanding of the Christian life. "I desire mercy, and not sacrifice" (Matt. 9:13), Jesus quoted from Hosea, and this was taken to mean that before God, assuming responsibility for one's fellowmen outweighed running off on pilgrimage. Even Wycliffe, who followed Bradwardine's protest against Ockhamite voluntarism and who stressed the elect, predestined nature of the church, nevertheless spoke of each man having mercy on his own soul by repenting and mending his ways as against availing himself of the dubious benefits of the ecclesiastical cult. Erasmus' satiric attacks were directed against the popular superstitions—the pilgrimages, prayers to saints, bead-telling, and relic worship.

Protestantism, however, moved in a different direction. The gospel of God's promise was set over against the law of God's demands and threats. Salvation was not an earned status but a free gift. The whole scheme to amount to something before God, to save oneself by either works of charity or cultic practices, was condemned as unbiblical and unchristian. Consequently, Reformation theology frequently was a polemic against voluntaristic schemes of salvation whether specifically Roman or not. The memory of that struggle has remained with Protestantism ever since, so that there is no going back to its sources which does not reengage the conflict between works and faith.

But too often faith itself was regarded as the work most pleasing to God. Protestant orthodox scholasticism in emphasizing the significance of right belief by its emphasis on correct doctrine derived directly from the Scriptures turned in this direction. In its crudest form it gave rise to the popular notion that one merits salvation by believing the right things, and the more impossible such right things may seem, the more merit there is in believing them—a notion still subject to the whole nominalistic dialectic of salvation and the Christian life.

A protest stemming from direct Bible study against this peculiar form of works righteousness led to the tendency to speak of things to believe and things to do as necessities for salvation. John Locke, at the end of the seventeenth century, reached the conclusion that the only "article of faith" that the New Testament requires is that Jesus is the Messiah (or Son of God, to use the equivalent term). But the New Testament also demands obedience to Jesus as Lord, God promising in the covenant of faith to make up the difference between our actual obedience, when we do our best, and his eternal standard of righteousness.[2]

Locke's protest against the notion of faith as "believing things" was carried far beyond his simplification by the Deists who saw the entire superstructure of positive doctrines, as against "natural religion," as but another form of medieval superstition. Their emphasis on responsible life in human society is to be seen in the whole perspective in which Kant wrote his *Religion within the Limits of Reason Alone,* a book which has served as a pattern (frequently unacknowledged and often unconsciously) for many expositions of the Christian life ever since.

If, for the Reformers, salvation is effected by Jesus Christ's work as Savior, sanctification must be something different from a remolding of character by an inner stiffening of the will to be righteous—self-righteous. Rather than being a requirement set either before or after the restoration to God's favor in justification, it is inseparably joined to justification as the manifestation of the new reality of Christ. And the faith necessary to justification is the utter trust of God who has shown himself trustworthy in Jesus Christ. This new reality effects both a mortification and a vivification, a dying and a being made alive—*together with Christ.*

At this point lies a difficulty, though, for while the dying and being made alive is visible, it cannot be equated with the accomplishment of any specific program of reform. As Augustine put it so many centuries ago, love feeds the hungry, but so does pride. Love gives its body to be burned, but so does pride.[3] There is no infallible test which will distinguish true love. Yet love does feed the hungry, tend the sick, visit the prisoner, and so forth. It is this very recognition that the Christian life is more than such specific acts that has provided the perennial resistance to the ethical reduction of faith.

The distinction between man's life before God and before men, which Luther so explicitly outlined in his early lectures on the epistle to the Romans, is still pertinent.

It is possible for a man to be righteous as judged in human society and still be a sinner as judged by God. The reverse also may be true. (The "Jews" of John's Gospel could say categorically even of Jesus, "We know that this man is a sinner," John 9:24.) In fact, every man righteous before God is so only by faith, so that he is also at the same time a sinner. Only after physical death is the dichotomy resolved. Because man cannot please God through some set of religious duties, he can live intelligently and responsibly in human society. Since his salvation is given him, he lives in that new reality, concerning himself with the needs of his neighbor. His inveterate self-interest spells out his neighborly responsibilities since he is now free to serve his neighbor as formerly he was bound to serve himself.

Traditional Lutheranism with its slogan of "justification by faith" looked askance at programs of self-improvement and community welfare so far as their significance for salvation was concerned. Kierkegaard was no spokesman for traditional Lutheranism, but his "knight of faith" or "inwardness" is a case in point.[4] Faith's inwardness gives no outward manifestation, otherwise faith has lost its unique dimension and has become instead only aesthetic affectation. To join together "without me you can do nothing" (John 15:5), with an outing to the Deer Park—that is the task of the Christian.[5] Kierkegaard protested any equating of Christianity with daily life in nineteenth-century Denmark. He spoke appreciatively of medieval monasticism for at least trying to take Christian discipleship seriously, although it gave discipleship a totally inadequate expression.

Lutheran Scandinavia, on the other hand, pioneered the creation of the "welfare state," but from the standpoint of the nature and responsibility of the state itself. The Swedish church, for example, did not regard this development as the valid expression of Christian life and resisted the legislation which brought it about.[5a] As secularization in the nineteenth century made the hope for a heavenly salvation incomprehensible, "bourgeois Christianity," with its pallid assumption that the Christian goal in human society had been reached or at least was not far off, was the result. The lack of any genuinely transcendent reference in bourgeois Christianity made an easy peace with the prevailing culture possible, so that to be a Christian came to mean to be a respectable member of a moderately progressive society. For many today this is still the important meaning of being a Christian.

In German thought, the ambiguous meanings of *Geist* ("spirit," "mind") and *geistlich* furthered the confusion between Christian faith and a culture centered in an idealistic metaphysic. The tragic consequence of this movement is seen but not exhausted in the "German Christianity" of the Nazi period. This nightmare led Bonhoeffer to challenge the whole picture of Kierkegaard's "knight of inwardness."[6] On the one hand, there was the impotence of cultural Christianity to challenge its culture, for it had lost the stance by which alone such criticism would be possible. And on the other hand, the knight of faith, recognizing faith to be something totally different from bourgeois Christianity, but giving no outward indication of his intense inwardness for fear of aestheticizing religion, could offer no resistance either, except as he was prompted by purely humanitarian motives. The resulting impasse is illustrated by the railroad dispatcher whose "Christian" life expressed itself in finding quicker routes for delivering seized Jews to Nazi death camps! These demonic tendencies of cultural Christianity lie in

the background of Bonhoeffer's *The Cost of Discipleship*
of the '30s. The beginning of the book protests the "cheap
grace" of far too much contemporary Christianity which
either uncritically blesses the unchristian culture or grants
individuals plenary absolution for their participation in
it.[7] The trouble with the monastery is not its demand for
separation from the world but the fact that it too is only
another part of the world.

SANCTIFICATION AS WORLD-TRANSFORMATION

A different emphasis is found in the Calvinistic strain of
Reformed thinking. Here too there is protest against medieval schemes of buying one's way before God. But joined
to the radical emphasis on God's justification expressed in
terms of divine election is the emphasis on sanctification.
"There is no confidence in God where there is no love of
righteousness," Calvin says categorically in the commentary on Romans. "Let believers, therefore learn to embrace
Him [Christ], not only for justification, but also for sanctification, as He has been given to us for both these purposes, that they may not rend Him asunder by their own
mutilated faith."[8] The thought goes back certainly to
Augustine, who was one of the first fathers to see the implications of the Christian life as a process of growth rather
than a being launched into the orbit of total Christianity
by the Sacrament of Baptism.

What Calvin specifically says about sanctification is intimately tied to his discussion of faith[9] of which one per-
ceptive student remarked, "He had to bleed to be able to
write that!" Faith, he says, is not a simple once-for-all affirmation, but a constant struggle with unbelief in which
—by God's grace—one nevertheless continues to cry,
"Abba, Father." Sanctification, then, is both mortification

and vivification. The dying to self is not the obliteration of personality, which some have misunderstood the mystics' quest to be, but the elimination of everything in the personality setting itself in opposition to God. Vivification is being made alive in Christ, a genuine transformation of life, though this objective change can in no way become an independent assurance of how things stand between men and God. There is no assurance in this life which can bypass faith, although later Calvinistic theologies were prone to regard the conquest of sin and even prospering in the world as signs of the Lord's favor.

The implications of sanctification were drawn out in the theologies of experience that constituted the evangelical "branch" of Calvinism in the seventeenth century. This is, properly speaking, the core of *Puritan* theology, but the Puritans have been spoken about so improperly in our time that one hesitates to risk the prejudging of the theology by attaching to it so prejudiced a label. For the Puritan of the seventeenth century, theology is a practical rather than a theoretical discipline. Theology deals with life from the "first conversion" in which the heart of stone is replaced by a heart of flesh and one is made ready to listen to Christ the teacher, until the lost image of God is again retraced in man. Although the Puritans wrote formal theology aplenty, the bulk of their theologizing took the form of spiritual diaries and biographies in which the process of transformation could be witnessed to and all its spurious imitations be detected and rejected. The honesty and candor of these diaries is enough in itself to shatter the stereotype of "Puritan" in our time.

This transformation was not a hoisting of oneself to heaven by one's bootstraps. But it did come from a recognition that the Christian life is not a matter of relaxa-

tion but of struggle.[10] When the struggle stops, the life is
all too likely to have died. Yet even dissatisfaction with
what one is is the sign—the "smoking flax"—of a light
that comes only from Christ, never from the devil. "Sin-
ners in the hands of an angry God" must be balanced by
the themes of consolation and encouragement preached
from such texts as Isa. 42:3 and John 6:37 for a true view
of Puritan preaching.

Because the Christian life is a struggle, one must use all
available help. Beginning with the definition of the church
as the communion of saints and emphasizing the aspect of
communion, the Puritan sought to build up the body of
Christ. Some have spoken of the effort as a lay monasticism,
a fleeing the world within the world. From this recognition that Christians must bind themselves together not
only for mutual encouragement but in expression of the
real life in Christ developed a host of practices familiar
today—the traditional picture of the Reformed pastor, the
emphasis on religious nurture in the home, the religious
societies of people who shared similar interests and problems.

The resources for this life are the Word of God and
prayer. Word of God includes, of course, the Sacraments
of Baptism and the Lord's Supper along with preaching
and study of Scripture in church life. But the Sacraments
were not understood as the means whereby supernatural
grace is infused into the believer, providing him with
supernatural power to reach his supernatural goal. Rather,
they testify to Christ's presence in the believing community, so that strength comes not from the Sacrament per
se but from the personal fellowship with the risen Lord
in the community of believers: "Christ in you, the hope
of glory" (Col. 1:27). And while the Bible in preaching

and study provides specific instruction which dare not be neglected, its primary purpose is to bring the believer into confrontation with Christ.

Prayer roots knowledge in the heart. Calvin frequently refers to his apt distinction between the "top of the head" and the "bottom of the heart." Nothing is to be found in the heart which has not gotten there somehow through the head. But the path from the head to the heart is prayer because in prayer the inmost core of the person is consciously open to God and the resources that he provides for his children on earth. There is no doubt in Calvin's mind that through prayer we are in fellowship with him who controls all things, for to be a Christian is to have to deal ultimately with a heavenly Father and not Stoic fate. But this does not make prayer some sort of magical incantation which can continually tamper with the order of things. For him there is no impersonal order of things set over against Christ and the believer.

It was largely through this tradition and its Continental counterpart of Pietism with its Lutheran roots, the two stimulating each other, that John Wesley came to develop his own emphasis of the Christian life. Wesley's personal history reflects the several stages of his understanding. During his student days at Oxford there was his first "conversion" (if one may call it that) to a serious concern with the Christian life. Patterned along the lines of traditional piety as expressed by William Law in *Christian Perfection* or *A Serious Call to a Devout and Holy Life,* or Jeremy Taylor's *Holy Living and Holy Dying,* it formed the basis of the "holy club" whose members were nicknamed the "methodists." Intense cultivation of the inner life through Bible study, prayer, introspection, group confession, and rigorous self-discipline was joined to outward service to others—feeding the hungry, tending the sick, visiting prisoners, and urging on all the serious matter of eternal salvation.

The second stage was marked by the strong influence of the Moravians with their emphasis on faith alone, an influence that led up to the "Aldersgate experience" in which Wesley came to know that he did trust God alone for salvation and that his sins had been taken away. It marked a turning point in his life as he saw that God did not require placating but gave what he asked. But Wesley's contacts with the group in England became clouded more and more by their antinomian tendencies. They set faith alone over against not only the attempts to buy one's way with God, but the very means by which God speaks with men: Bible study, prayer, worship, and the Sacraments. The righteousness of faith was held to be so contrary to any inherent righteousness of the Christian himself that any *development* of the Christian life was denied. One was not a Christian until he had faith, Wesley's Moravian friends argued, and nothing he could do might procure it for him. With faith he had everything.

The months and years following Aldersgate then found Wesley moving away from this understanding of the Christian life toward that of classical Puritanism. Is love only imputed to the Christian, asked Wesley, or does the Christian really love God and man? Is chastity only imputed to the Christian, or is he really chaste?[11] Because God himself is at work the Christian is enabled to will and to work. Therefore faith does not supplant human effort but makes it possible and gives it significance. (Phil. 2:12–13). The life of faith is a development of real righteousness looking toward being made perfect in love of God and one's fellowman. This is the work of God. The wholeness to which

God restores the sinner in Christ is not only an abstract "spiritual" status but the divine image traced again in the very being of man. Therefore the Christian must concern himself with "spreading scriptural holiness throughout the land."

In this way the Christian life has legitimate social and personal implications. Any social service is undertaken, not just for the spiritual discipline which it provides the believer as he strives for his own perfection, so that it is a sort of by-product of his personal quest for salvation, but for the sake of all men whom God himself loves and to whom he ministers through concerned believers. And on the other hand, salvation is not concerned solely with either a transcendent "heaven" or an eschatological age to come, but with the real personalities, characters, and mutual relationships of those who are being saved. It is not a question of believing more firmly because external buttresses of a better personal character or a more just social order have been added to God's own witness to himself through the Spirit. It is rather a matter of enjoying what the Scriptures have promised. For Christian doctrine, according to Wesley, tells us who the Christian is, promises its realization, and then shows how it becomes reality in life.[12] The Christian is one who loves God with all his heart, mind, soul, and strength, and his neighbor as himself. To be saved is so to love God and neighbor. The Christian life is learning so to love.

SANCTIFICATION SECULARIZED

Since the eighteenth century, the intellectual problems that tormented Christian theology have shifted the emphasis to aesthetics or ethics in such a way that the Christian life has become radically subjectivized. The questionable linking of theology to metaphysics in the seventeenth century threw theology into confusion when attention shifted from metaphysics to history. The picture of the total order that God was realizing—an order engrained in the very nature of things—began to fade, and in its place came an emphasis on what one personally could do or could appropriate to himself by way of spiritual development. Only *spiritual*, instead of referring to God's Spirit, was now understood as a dimension of humanity itself.

Christian theology has always kept up a dialogue with "secular" philosophy for two reasons. In the first place there is the question of the *language* in which the gospel is to be expressed. As has been pointed out *ad nauseam* in our age, a message can be understood only if it is set in understandable language. But a language is more than merely words used—as any student of a foreign language can testify to his distress. It involves the ways these words are put together, not simply in grammatical constructions, but in relation to the whole culture. Philosophy is a culture reflecting on itself, trying to understand itself, trying to explain its language. Hence, its first significance to theology.

In the second place there is the question of the *truth claims* of a philosophy—that is, of the culture itself from which the philosophy has developed. As Hegel put it well over a century ago, a philosophy without a metaphysic is like a religion without a Holy of Holies. A philosophy that stops short of the problem of God is only a dilettante philosophy. But when the gospel confronts philosophy on this level and not merely on the level of language, the problems of theology are compounded. All too easily theology is then absorbed into philosophy, or rather into a particular philosophy, which makes its coming to terms with a wholly different culture traumatic and perilous. Christian theology of the Middle Ages, for example, was identified with medieval culture in a way different from that relation in the early centuries of the church. Thus the collapse of medieval culture could not be witnessed by theology with tranquillity, even by those leading the Reformation. The lingering influence of nominalism was neither easily nor quickly transcended.

For John Locke, the cosmological argument which preoccupied Christian apologetics in spite of Duns Scotus' and Ockham's questioning of it was based on the human self-consciousness rather than on the certain and objective existence of the world as such. The development of science in the Renaissance had raised the question about the nature of the "real" world in a radical form. About all one could say of the world was that it was amenable to man's scientific explanation and manipulation. But it was no longer clear which qualities characterized the world as such and which belonged to the minds of its human observers. Certainty could no longer rest with "the world" but had to find its foundation in man's own consciousness.

Kant insisted that it is impossible to argue from the existence of the fact of the world to God because the categories of rational understanding apply only within the world and cannot be extended beyond it. Nor does the existence of a world apparently organized in many respects around purposes prove a divine mind of Christian proportions because there is too much evidence of chaos and even of demonic dispurpose to draw any binding conclusion. We have no "experience" of God, Kant held, because our *total* experience gives us only "the world," although that world may have strange and wonderful dimensions.

Yet what Kant took away with one hand he restored

with the other. God, who was bereft of theoretical foundation, was a necessary postulate of practical reason. To make
possible man's moral life (in which he is called to fulfill
his own uniqueness which sets him off from all creatures
of necessity) one must presuppose freedom (the possibility
of choosing, which theoretical reason operating in the con-
fines of determinism could not demonstrate), immortality
(as an infinite growing together of the moral law and human conduct), and God (who was the ground of freedom
and immortality). God thereby became the great "As If"
since man must live "as if" God is, if he is to fulfill his
unique capacity as a *person*.

The traditional order of Reformation thought has been
reversed. *There* it was God's action which made the new
life possible. *Here* the possibility of the new life—which
is a genuinely *human* possibility—permits as well as requires the inference to God. In the attempt to relate the
divine and human in man and his choices, God has become
only a way of speaking about the human possibility.

Kant did not stop there, however, for in his third great
critique, the *Critique of Judgment,* he explored man's
aesthetic response to the world. Kant is careful to point out
that the conclusions reached in this investigation dare not
be confused with those reached by theoretical reason. We
are not speaking of the world as it is in itself, but as it is
for us in those dimensions of sensitivity which are not immediately subject to scientific investigation. All men experience beauty which strikes them as though some purpose that they had formulated had been fulfilled, though
they had actually formulated none. They know also the
sublime, the sense of wonder at the limitless, the sense of
dread at what transcends finite dimensions (though still
within this world). Since no purpose has been formulated
for which these experiences are the fulfillment, and since

the human mind cannot project a future fulfillment as the "cause" of events contributing to it save as it is already a purpose in the mind of an active intelligence, we are driven to speak of God who has thus organized the world as to make possible aesthetic experience. In other words, here a teleology is introduced which cannot be justified by theoretical reason.

Before one seizes on such a teleology and argument, however, he must be aware of their implications. Kant said that two things filled him with religious awe: the moral law within and the starry heavens above. By the latter he referred to the thought we have just outlined, not to the classical teleological argument as it comes to us from Plato or Aristotle. God, in other words, has become a useful way of speaking of our human experience. God is a means of self-realization. Christian life is not a flight from the world, not the sojourn of a heaven-bound pilgrim, but a development of one's human potentialities in an ever deeper involvement in the world.

Sanctification thereby has become a doctrine of progress concerning the world itself. If the supernatural reference of life is removed and one has the single dimension of this world, then one can speak only of a change in one's inner motivation or of outward behavior. Service to one's fellowmen is directed toward a more adequate meeting of human needs through improved social institutions. Thus, at the same time that the scope of neighbor love is extended to the whole human community, sanctification becomes a community process. In this development, the goal of sanctification is shifted to the realization of human potentiality defined in this-worldly terms. "Love of God" then becomes an epiphenomenon of feeling, a sort of aesthetic coloring to a reality which takes no note of it.

Carl Becker has commented on how the traditional

heaven or City of God became posterity for the eighteenth-century philosophers.[13] On the one hand, there is in this a loss of the earlier orientation directed toward the destiny of each man's immortal soul. But on the other hand, there is the recognition that such personal development takes place only in a social context. Not only do good people form a good society but a good society is requisite for the growth of good people. But objective action in the world is governed by purely immanental factors. One asks such questions as: "Does it contribute to the greatest happiness of the greatest number?" "Does it fit in with human development?" As sociological and psychological data become available, the human adaptation becomes all the more realistically oriented. It is assumed that man, simply as a member of the human community, is concerned for its welfare, recognizing from mounting knowledge that his own personal welfare is one with the welfare of the community.

If this then is the context of life—the human community with its own needs but also with its own inner direction—what place does Christianity have? With these assumptions it can have one of two places: either it is simply identified with the ongoing process of human community or else it becomes the area of inner response, feeling, or attitude. With the second alternative, one can choose either Kant's ethical or Schleiermacher's aesthetic version. That is, Christianity can be identified with an inner willingness to go along with the insights that our natural and human sciences provide as against a recognition that desires and knowledge conflict. Kant laid his emphasis on the maxim by which one acted, knowing that the same outward act could be prompted by any one of a number of different and even conflicting maxims. Christianity, insofar as he could understand it, "real" Christianity as against the superstitious accretions of the Middle Ages, is acting from the sense of what is right in itself as against the play for power, quest for pleasure, or desire for applause. "God's will" is only another form which this genuinely human phenomenon can take. Thus only the person himself could know whether his act was religious in the only valid sense. The communal aspects of sanctification are transferred to the natural human order and so are secularized while the personal, individual dimension alone remains religious.

The same thing happens in a different way in Schleiermacher's thought. He was loathe to identify religion with either ethics or philosophy per se and consequently he understood it to relate to the unique category of feeling. The link here to Kant's third critique is apparent. The particular feeling with which he is concerned is the sense of the infinite, or as he restated it in *The Christian Faith*, the feeling of total dependence, the higher self-consciousness.[14] Such feeling is shared by all men, but consciousness of it varies from next to nothing to a continuous awareness—as it was for Jesus Christ. One is a Christian insofar as his religious consciousness is increased by his relation to Jesus. The expression in human acts of this higher, religious self-consciousness gives rise, as do all common human factors, to the religious community, the church, which expresses its inner reality in liturgy, Scripture, and even technical theology. Without undervaluing this communal aspect of Christianity (for all language grows out of human community) one still must recognize that religion begins with a certain feeling tone. The possibility of such a feeling tone is inherent with all men, but its increase and cultivation can be encouraged by a community specifically devoted to this purpose. Here again, the peculiarly religious dimensions of sanctification have no direct relation to human activity. Presumably there is no outward change at all but only a change in one's feeling in regard to it all. One can be—as the once-popular book title had it—"in tune with the infinite."

In summary we can point out that the changes in human relationships which were traditionally directly tied to Christian obedience to Jesus Christ in faith have now become the province of nonreligious human concerns; and what now is understood to be the proper province of Christianity is man's inner life—his attitudes and feelings. Christians are of course concerned with human welfare and justice, but really as members of the human community itself and not because of particular Christian commitment.

Developments subsequent to Kant and Schleiermacher continued in the same direction. The *human* truth of the Christian man rests upon other than Christian foundations. And Christian truth then becomes an optional overtone to humanity in general. For Hegel, Christianity is an intuitive grasp of the direction in which the human community must move, but on its own foundation and reason. For Ritschl, who is primarily Kantian in sympathy, Christianity affirms the priority of human spirit over matter and delivers men from the crippling sense of guilt which restrains their efforts for human community. In both cases Christian sanctification has become universalized. The Christian shaping of life is identical with the program of this world's wisdom. The problem of the supernatural origin of Christianity disappears along with its supernatural goal. There is no longer a need for miracle as the point of contact between two quite different orders. There is only one world order in process and the completion of this process (as an eschatological goal since the process and the development can go on ad infinitum) is identified with what Christians for years have talked about as sanctification, insofar as that was not confined purely to a concern with personal character in an alien world.

We have said that where religion still had a place in the thought of the nineteenth century, that place was purely in personal, inner response to the world—a "feeling" of satisfaction, rightness, harmony with the depth of life. But this area too became secularized in several ways. For Freud, God is simply a human creation—not necessarily a conscious fabrication, but a manipulation by which men have avoided a threatening psychotic aspect of life. "God" saves us from being overwhelmed by the natural order. As such, God is an *illusion* for Freud, not from the standpoint of its truth or falsity, but only from the standpoint of its origin. But the whole phenomenon has been caught up in the father-complex of threat and protection. Now men of insight can see through the illusion, and the future development of man depends upon his shaking himself loose from this illusion to use the new tools that science has given him for meeting the problems of life, the problems from which "God" once provided a safe refuge. This simply means that the problems of personal response to reality, which had been retained within the "religious" area when the objective elements were transferred to the secular realm, have also come under the control of a secular technique—in this case, psychoanalysis and therapy.

A similar development took place earlier with Karl Marx who had had enough "explaining" the world and now, in face of the plight of the mid-nineteenth-century European working class, wanted to change it. Thus far there is an interest akin to Christian intention. But for Marx, religion was one of the factors preventing change by relieving the pressure of demand for change in other-worldly hopes and internalized personal developments. In other words, instead of demanding reform of intolerable conditions, the abused man was taught by religion to develop personal qualities of resignation and patience in his plight. When actual conditions were changed, this sort of "escapist" response was unnecessary and therefore religion —including Christianity—was unnecessary.

The Recovery of a Christian Meaning

In this context of secularization such otherwise diverse theologians as Barth and Tillich have sought to restore meaning to sanctification. Both are aware, as the eighteenth-century theologians often were not, of its corporate, social dimensions. Both recognize that *humanitas* is not simply a generic term applicable only to individuals but rather incorporates a dimension realizable only in community. And both recognize that sanctification is more than society projecting its ideals. Tillich speaks of the ambiguity of cultural manifestations, Barth of the sinfulness in which everything human participates. Both see in Christ the new humanity in which all men are called to live.

Karl Barth stresses that sanctification is contained within the incarnation: the humiliation of the Son of God is one with the exaltation of the Son of Man. In Jesus Christ, God goes into the far country and man returns home.[15] As God "turns to man in defiance of his sin He also, in defiance of his sin, turns man to Himself."[16] Any attempt to break up this one reality into chronological stages of salvation must be resisted because it can only result in the travesty which Bonhoeffer labeled "cheap grace." "We have only to ask

ourselves: What is the forgiveness of sins (however we understand it) if it is not directly accompanied by an actual
liberation from the committal of sin? What is divine sonship if we are not set in the service of God and the brethren? . . . What is faith without obedience?"[17] On the other
hand, there is no base for this new action apart from justification.

Barth emphasizes that sanctification means that God
creates for himself a holy people and that therefore the
Christian life is not our own independent response to forgiveness but rather is itself an aspect of Christ's total work.
The Christian life is "participating in Christ," to use a
favorite phrase of John Calvin's. Such participation is not
a matter of arbitrary choice on an individual's part. Every
man is ordained to the new humanity of the Son of God.
"To say God the Father, Son, and Holy Ghost is to say
also the awakening of man to conversion."[18]

The concrete working out of this new humanity is
through the call to discipleship which is life of obedience
but not to a "program." "The commanding grace of God,
and therefore salvation as Jesus' call to discipleship," Barth
writes, "never come into the life of a man in such a way
that he is given leave to consider why and how he may
best follow the command given. The command given is
recognizable as the command of Jesus by the fact that it is
quite unambiguous."[19] This command entails a historical
and visible break with the past and enrollment in the
militia Christi to fight not a world of non-Christians but
against one's own commitment to "Lord Everyman." Its
decisive expression is not cult but the whole man. Yet it is
also this whole man who is bound by sin. Barth rejects
any concept of sanctification which projects an enlarging
proportion of the new man to the old in the life of the

Christian. But neither will he condone a theology which minimizes the power of grace. Man has no future in sin: his future is in Christ alone.

The contrast of Paul Tillich's language of the idealistic tradition to Barth's words almost belies the fact that they both claim to be speaking about the same reality. For Tillich, sanctification is the movement toward unambiguous manifestations of the spirit. Spirit (spelled with a small *s*) is the dimension of self-transcendence, the "more than" biological or psychical existence without being itself another "thing." It is a dimension (rather than level) of existence appearing noticeably only in man and expressing itself in his morality, culture, and religion. But all historical manifestations of self-transcendence (spirit) are ambiguous—which means that they raise as many questions as they answer. How can agape love, for example, be a moral norm when it is always bound with human libido in particular expressions?[20] How can any particular command be categorically imperative?

The unity and wholeness of human persons, for Tillich, points to a fundamental unity of reality. The unity of the divine center manifested as "Spiritual Presence" is the source of the integration of human centers, but not as a cause among causes. Rather, it is "present" to all causes. The action of "Spiritual Presence" can then be described as healing or salvation, a restoring of wholeness to which spirit itself points. In fact, the term Spirit (spelled with a capital *S*) is a symbol, derived from experience of the human spirit. Eternal life is the "inner aim" of all creatures, their fulfillment in God.[21] "God, so to speak, drives toward the actualization and essentialization of everything that has being."[22]

Christ then is understood as the manifestation of the "New Being" in which these ambiguities of spirit are conquered. The reality of Christ, for Tillich, includes mankind itself as the locus in spirit of the manifestation of the divine Spirit, the central manifestation of the Spirit (albeit hidden except to faith) in Jesus, and the Spiritual community brought into existence by that central manifestation.[23] Sanctification is the appearance of the New Being as the community bearing the same marks manifested in Jesus— healthy wholeness—on the ground of faith by which finite spirit is bound to divine Spirit. Tillich points out that the Spiritual community is not to be identified with the ambiguity-ridden historical churches.

Although Barth and Tillich see part of their function as theologians as correcting errors in the light of the authentic Biblical message, they are nevertheless children of their own times—much more so than is often superficially apparent.

CHAPTER II

The Demand for Reinterpretation

If there is one common theme running through nearly all the current discussions of the Christian life, it is that somehow the period in which we now live is separated by a watershed from all that has gone before. There is always change from one generation to another as the same fundamental principles are adapted to new situations. But current talk involves more than this. It calls for and tries to provide a radical rethinking of what it means to be a Christian and to live as a Christian. Conscious of the sheer inertia of human nature, Christians have always understood the value of exhortation and encouragement. But whereas these in the past have usually met with the response: "You're right. I should live this way," now the response is more likely to be a baffled: "This no longer makes sense to me. Even to what I regard as my Christian conscience it does not make sense."

Compare, for example, Dietrich Bonhoeffer's earlier book, *The Cost of Discipleship,* with his remarks in *Letters and Papers from Prison.* One might say that the earlier book, built around the thesis *"Only he who believes is obedient, and only he who is obedient believes,"*[1] is traditional in its orientation, even in attacking the distortions of Reformed doctrine that manifested themselves as "cheap grace." While there is in it a refreshing exegesis and application of those Biblical passages which constitute a "canon within the canon" for most Christians, there is nothing that one would regard as revolutionary in the sense of a contradiction or repudiation of traditional views. In fact, it could more readily be understood as an attack on contemporary forms of apostasy and unbelief that mask themselves with Christian respectability.

In *Letters and Papers from Prison*, however, although there is a good deal of the same sort of emphasis pointed up more sharply by references to his own daily experience and that of his nation's people, there are notes of a much more radical sort of thought. Just how radical is a matter of dispute, for some have taken what Bonhoeffer raised as questions to be the substance of his thinking. One cannot know how a living Bonhoeffer might have developed or repudiated his prison meditations in the light of the events since that time.

The time of inwardness and conscience, along with the time when theology could supply answers for everything, is over, he says. "We are proceeding towards a time of no religion at all: men as they are now simply cannot be religious anymore."[2] Referring to Karl Barth's distinction between religion as men's attempts to build their own way to God and Christianity as the true religion of God's coming to man in Jesus Christ, he raises the question whether man is inherently religious at all or whether he simply passed through a religious stage in his history: "If we reach the stage of being radically without religion—and I think this is more or less the case already, else how is it, for instance, that this war, unlike any of those before it, is not calling forth any 'religious' reaction?—what does that mean for 'Christianity'?"[3]

If this is the case, he continues, then we must inquire as

to the role of the church, the meaning of God, the place of the devotional life, and so forth, in such an age of no religion. *Religious* people have a God who is really a *deus ex machina*, that is, a God who provides the answers for human questions. But God's "beyondness" (transcendence) is something we rather meet, if we meet it at all, in the center and not on the fringes of life.

Again, to speak "religiously" is to speak either metaphysically or individualistically. But neither is relevant to the Biblical message or to contemporary man.[4] "Man has learned to cope with all questions of importance without recourse to God as a working hypothesis."[5] Christian apologetic too often has tried to reverse the trend by counteracting man's self-assurance. Bonhoeffer reproves the existentialists and psychotherapists for trying "to drive men to inward despair."[6] But what is Christ's place in this new world? That is, what place does he take, not to what place does the world assign him?[7] Religion must not be made a precondition of faith![8] Faith springs from the wealth and depth of the world, not from its cares and longings.[9]

Although one can both argue with Bonhoeffer's interpreters and protest the appropriateness of his reflections, there is no question but that in these words he speaks for a good many thinking men, including Christians, in his recognition that man is not now religiously oriented in the same way that he was in past ages. Mircea Eliade, not a theologian but a student of the history of religions, has argued that modern man is distinguished from his predecessors by the fact that he lacks the cosmological orientation in space and time which religion once provided. The sacred has been displaced by the secular, in other words, except in man's subconscious where it breaks to the surface only in dreams and gives the objects of daily life unique hidden meanings.[10] Building on suggestions voiced in the nineteenth century, many today have said in various senses (some of which are mutually contradictory) that "God is dead." Although the doctrine of God is to be dealt with in another volume of this series, we cannot understand present thought in regard to the Christian life unless we keep in mind at least the main channels of the development leading up to it. The Christian life may be something quite different if the traditional setting of God and his will changes.

THE QUESTION OF GOD

The phenomenon which Bonhoeffer discusses might be illustrated by a recent documentary film on the perennial food crisis in southeast Asia. Bound by ignorance and cultural pressures to the agricultural methods of his forebears, the native farmer of the region is pictured tilling, planting, cultivating, and harvesting his fields in traditional ways that cannot possibly increase his food supply. In the face of a growing population's demand for food, he has no recourse but to supplicate the gods for help. Against that hopelessness, however, is pictured the application of modern agricultural techniques developed by research and experimentation. Power tilling, hybrid seeds, chemical fertilizers, insecticides, mechanical harvesting, processing, and transporting equipment—these reliably produce much higher yields from the same land area. While the purpose of the film is to indicate the role of agricultural missions in meeting the world food crisis, it illustrates poignantly the lesson that men in our age are learning: human need is met by scientific knowledge and technology, not by religion. It is not likely today that men would hesitate in choosing between prayer and faith on the one hand and vaccines, antibiotics, and modern surgery on the other in the interest of health.

With the shift from Aristotelian to modern science, God is no longer reckoned with as a force in the world. In the older science, *understanding* was itself understood teleologically. When one said he *understood* something, he meant he could relate it to a purpose that it fulfilled. All partial purposes were integrated in the final purpose or end—God. One could not understand this world apart from the reference to God. The purpose of God was the most important "cause" with which one had to deal.

Understanding, however, came to have a different meaning in modern science. It was no longer oriented toward purpose. For Newton and Galileo, one *understood* a process when one could relate various stages of its continuing motion to each other. The relevant elements of this sort of understanding were mathematical entities: time, distance, mass. Things could be explained in terms of themselves, not in relation to God. One no longer had to take God and his purpose into account in explaining a natural event—or in dealing with it for that matter. In terms of this new framework, if God were to show himself as *causing* some event in the natural order, it could only be as a violation or a setting aside of that order.

This explains the peculiar emphasis placed on miracles by those in the seventeenth and eighteenth centuries who were trying to maintain the significance of God in the lives of men. Only in a miracle could he squeeze into this world! But he did so only in the interest of salvation. Miracles were thought to confirm revealed doctrine. But as for the daily course of events, Laplace could say that he had no need for the God-hypothesis; i.e., things can be explained satisfactorily without making reference to God. Even God as "first cause" was no longer necessary, because it was just as reasonable to posit an eternal motion of matter as an eternal God.

In the face of this baffling inability to root God in the metaphysical structure of reality, another avenue of theology was explored—the ethical. That is, the *function* of God, it was alleged, is not to give an accounting of things but to help men live in the right way. Theology is practical, not theoretical. It has to do with life, not an abstract order of being. While the debate about the real nature of theology has run throughout its history, the metaphysical impasse of the eighteenth century threw attention to ethics in a radical way. It had the effect of making God a human creation. God stands in the shadows, as it were, as a guarantor of the moral order, but he does not enter into human affairs. Since he does not belong in any way to the order of cause and effect, he can "cause" nothing, not even a change in the mind of a man, except that by meditating on God a man may keep his mind on the rational ideal of duty and act in response to its demands. But one can do things and accomplish goals only as he sets in motion the relevant elements of the whole causal order of which God is not a part. Religion is no resource in the course of things.

In this development, "God" and the language of religion have become but another vocabulary in which the reality of the human situation can be expressed. It is possible, therefore, to translate it into other terms. Liberal theology of the first part of the twentieth century was fond of speaking of the "infinite worth of human personality." This was the Ritschlian appropriation of the categorical imperative which for Kant was the source of all valid speaking about

God. To say it is to say that human personality is God. A less revealing way of putting it is to say that faith in God involves faith in the superiority of man's spirit over matter, the superiority of value over fact.

But there are dimensions of human experience that resist incorporation into this sort of scheme: a sense of kinship and immediate reality rather than an inference or conclusion drawn from some other sort of reality. The Romantics of the eighteenth and nineteenth centuries thought of God not as another way of speaking but as a pervasive "presence" in all experience, the "sense sublime of something far more deeply interfused."[11] Schleiermacher claimed this specifically for religion in his identification of God with the source of our feeling of *total* dependence underlying our ordinary experiences of partial dependence and partial freedom. With such a view, there was no need for miracle to announce God's presence because he was in everything as its ground. The problem with such a view, however, is that the lesson to be learned from "everything" is ambiguous.

If God is such an all-pervading being ("panentheism" is the term often used), how does one become conscious of him? If God is the constant factor in every moment, how is he to be recognized? The answer many gave was that he could be known in those "frontier" experiences of life in which one is confronted by his own limitations. In every moment man is dependent upon God, but only when human resources are lacking does he recognize this measure of dependence. It is not that God can answer for the gaps in human knowledge and technique, but that when those gaps are met, one somehow is aware of the divine presence.

But when God is understood as the whole of things as their ultimate ground (as with Paul Tillich's "ground of being" or "being itself"), then the question is not when or where he makes himself known—for that is everywhere and at all times. The question is how men understand and represent to each other that primal reality. This approach in the nineteenth century led to great interest in the history of religions, particularly in the evolution of the concept of God. In early stages of religion, natural objects sufficed. Later, human artistry was required in sculpture and painting. Still later, human activity had to be more directly incorporated in the expression in dance, drama, and liturgy. Finally, in Christianity the process was thought to have reached its goal. The ever enlarging factor of human subjecthood expressing itself in deeper and deeper forms of creativity acknowledged that only man himself in the full range of his being as subject can represent the truth of God. Hegel, who gave us this scheme of development, saw its culmination in the Christian doctrine of the incarnation which affirms the victory over alienation in the unity of God and man. He thought that religion, with its *representational* type of expression, opens new areas of understanding through intuition, but these must be mapped by philosophy in *conceptual* form.

But if religion, including the concepts of God, has thus undergone a development in history, it is conceivable that a postreligious stage might appear. The whole phenomenon of religion might belong to but one epoch of human history. Or, religious language may be figurative expression for some truth, an adequate understanding of which might supplant religion in human life. The "need" for God now is the need for an explanation or expression of a reality which remains whether it is explained or not. Such a need is a human emotional need, and while the power of emotion cannot be gainsaid, emotional needs sooner or later must be adjusted to the facts of the case. So, many insist that man must grow up to face reality without the crutches of religion, for he can learn to live creatively and happily in a "godless" world.

Ludwig Feuerbach took this position in the mid-nineteenth century and insisted that Christian theology was all true, but true of man rather than of some abstract being "God." Man had simply objectified his own ideal self. The worship of "God" is worship of the divine in man who is both *I* and *Thou*. If feeling is said to relate us to God, this can only mean that feeling itself is divine. God-talk indicates the supreme valuation of those things which are taken to be his attributes and qualities. Theology is all true when we recognize that its subject is man. The mistaken reference, however, has directed service from man himself to an illusion. Hence, the discovery of the true meaning of "God" now frees men of "religious" duties to serve each other and thereby realize the human potentialities once acknowledged only in the form of divine attributes.

A similar movement takes place in the thought of Søren Kierkegaard although his emphasis is different. Kierkegaard refused to make religion merely preliminary to some other discipline. Faith is not a school for numbskulls, he insisted. Nor is it an ephemeral overtone of all experience, as the Romantics held. Nor is it to be identified with ethics —reason's universal insights in the form of divine commands. The area of religion lies beyond all these as man must take upon himself the full responsibility of life before God. Thus religion involves a man not as the world involves him even in its most lofty dimensions, nor as a law universal to mankind, but in his individual existence. Man is called to risk everything—even the ethical—for God! But what is this God?

The existentialist appropriation of Kierkegaard has stressed "authentic existence," which means man's assuming full responsibility for his life as against being the product of external forces or the subject of universal laws. Some existentialists speak of God, but others insist that God—if the word is to have any real meaning—is only an escape from full individual authenticity. Certain Christian theologians such as Rudolf Bultmann and Friedrich Gogarten understand the language of the Bible and traditional theology as a mythological expression of such existential truth. "To objectify God and His Word is to deny Him," says Gogarten.[12] "God" can have nonmythological meaning as "ground of being" or "non-objective reality." Schubert Ogden, who uses the latter phrase, means by it something other than man himself and yet not an object to be observed, described, or analyzed.[13]

In contemporary life we are faced with the progressive removal of "God" from the realms of philosophy, science, ethics, and aesthetics. Paul van Buren asks if the time has not come to drop "God" from theology as well.[14] For "God" as the word is thus used is so eviscerated of former meanings as to be only confusing. If there is some dimension of experience which points to him—and for many today this is only *mystery*—this is of such a nature that it cannot be given systematic exposition but, as Pseudo-Dionysius said nearly fifteen centuries ago, can only be "celebrated" and referred to symbolically (poetically?) and negatively. There is no *knowledge* of such a God, however, which can be worked intelligibly into the wider scope of human knowledge. Human affairs must be evaluated, directed, and corrected by a quite different reference.

This position has also been taken by those influenced by the language-analysis school of philosophy. Beginning with

Wittgenstein's suggestion of the plurality of "language games" as a way out of the constrictions of older logical positivism, they have sought to analyze the peculiar use of theological language. But the insistence that mixing different kinds of language games into a single speech only leads to hopeless confusion underscores the isolation of "God" in contemporary thought. That is, he belongs to a particular aspect of life (one language game) and does not interact with the wider range of life's realities—unless there is some possibility of speaking of the interests of science, ethics, and politics in religious language. Professor William Hordern points out that the language game of theology belongs to a particular way of life, and that one can participate in the game only by participating in that way of life.[15]

A counter proposal to all this is the development of a reconstructed metaphysic. The abandonment of the metaphysical foundation for religion in the eighteenth century was itself abortive, it is held. It led theology into worse predicaments than those from which it sought to escape. While seventeenth-century metaphysics cannot be recalled to validity in the present day because of our expanded scientific knowledge, a new metaphysic, taking into account the developments, discoveries, and insights of the past three centuries, can be worked out. And therein lies the hope for making God relevant to an understanding of the world in its totality and thus for the Christian life. The loss of a sense of God's reality is not a matter of indifference to the Christian gospel, much less a gain for true Christianity.

John B. Cobb, Jr., one of the younger American theologians taking this stand, holds that the loss of the meaning of the word "God" has not come from deeper insight into

Christian faith but from a cosmology that has destroyed the context in which men, up to the most recent times, have understood their existence.[16] He contends that "a cosmology lacking the destructive implications of much modern cosmological thought is not only possible but also more adequate to the modern situation than its competitors."[17] He finds this in an adaptation of Whitehead's philosophy along lines suggested by Charles Hartshorne who thought to maintain God's relevance to the world by arguing for his interaction with the world. In other words, it is sought to make God once again a philosophically legitimate principle of explanation and not merely a pietistic premise.

Although the task of relating what Christianity speaks of as God to all other experience cannot be ignored, some attention must be given to what it speaks of in the way it speaks. The language is personal: God knows, hears, gives, promises, judges, forgives, remembers, and, mercifully, forgets. Our question focuses in the phenomenon of personality. Is the experience of confronting another person a unique dimension of experience or is it a conclusion drawn from a familiar concurrence of data which are in themselves impersonal? Certainly the usual experiences of personal presence are accompanied by visual phenomena which can be photographed, audio phenomena which can be recorded, and sensations of touch and smell which might be reproduced. In that sense, "person" is the term we give to a certain grouping of such physical data. If this were the case, one might mistake one of Walt Disney's intricate puppets used in certain displays of the New York World's Fair for a person. What would tell him that he was wrong in his assumption? Possibly the rather limited response of a programmed puppet, no matter how intricately designed, as against the more extended range of response of a living person. But is this all? Is personal presence no more than this or is it even completely dependent upon this? The last survivors of Scott's ill-fated expedition to the South Pole left records that they were aware of an additional "person" who had joined them, though there was none of the usual physical signs of such a person's presence. Many under normal conditions can relate similar experiences. In fact, some have said that it is a rare experience to feel *really* alone.

Can *God* be known in this way as well? Is "personal" only symbolic when used of God, so that because certain experiences are "like" those associated with human persons we speak of God as "person" though he really is something quite different—an idea in our minds? Is *personal* a symbol twice removed from God—from God to human persons, and from human persons to certain configurations of nonpersonal facts? Or is there an area where God speaks, confronts, engages?

Emil Brunner has defined theology as having to do with the divine confrontation. God meets us as a *thou* (to use a term derived from Ludwig Feuerbach, of all people, through Martin Buber). *He* meets us in the crisis of personal decision. But William Hamilton, educated in this theological framework, has said that he experiences only the absence of God instead of that confrontation.[18] That experience is not new, nor is it tied exclusively to the modern world view. The Bible speaks of a God who will reveal himself to whom he chooses to reveal himself. In these terms, personal confrontation cannot be made universal. Such a God is not simply a different name for an experience that is universal, so that men might be made believers by giving them a new vocabulary. Some have suggested that the sense of personal presence is characteristic of only certain types of the human psyche. Schleiermacher, in his early *Speeches,* said that some find it meaningful to use personal language in relation to God while others do not. Joseph Fletcher suggests that only "mystics and highly religious people" have a feeling for God's presence.[19] On the other hand, some suggest that people without this feeling do not know God, in spite of the concerns associated with God—love of fellowmen, concern for others, self-giving devotion—which they exemplify.

Does the Christian life require "God" as its foundation or can it have wide significance in an age for which "God" has become so problematic? Is there a Christian life which can move beyond "God—the problem"?

THE QUESTION OF CHRIST

Although Christian theology does not try to develop a doctrine of God *sui generis* from which it derives "signs of divinity" by which to test the life of Jesus Christ, there is no question but that the problems of speaking about God (especially those which lie beyond the mere use of words) have affected the contemporary understanding of Christ as well. On the other hand, the insights which have come in thinking about Christ, particularly in relation to his humanity, have crucially affected traditional thought about God. The dogmatic affirmation of Christ's humanity and divinity formulated at Chalcedon has been radically questioned insofar as it does not come to terms with the full dimension of *human* existence.

On the one hand, emphasis on the utter transcendence of God which denies his appearance as a cause among causes has made naïve concepts of the God-man more impossible than ever. The virgin birth, for example, cannot

be understood—if it ever was by responsible theologians
—as God's taking the initiative in the specific act of human
procreation. Chalcedon also denied this in saying that the
two natures were joined but not mixed or confused in
Christ. But on the other hand, emphasis on the total im-
manence of God has put the whole weight of Jesus'
uniqueness and significance on his human development,
his use of his human capacities, or upon his representative
status as "man" himself. All this is to say that somehow
the tension incorporated in the Chalcedonian formula has
been relaxed for many, either by denying one pole of the
two-nature scheme or by identifying God and man.

But Christology has also been affected by a change in the
understanding of what it means to be a man. From the
days of Augustine onward, considerable effort has been
made to explore and understand man from the standpoint
of *will* rather than *essence*. To be man is not simply to be
constituted of human stuff, but to think, choose, play,
hope, work, suffer, procreate—in short, to be involved in
the whole range of human responsibilities. And this problem of the will must be worked out not only in the dimension of Jesus Christ, but in the dimensions of our own
experience. In that sense, Christology has been bound up
with the whole problem of Christian anthropology. Karl
Barth's insistence that we must begin with Jesus Christ
for our understanding of man[20] is not completely helpful,
because we do not approach the New Testament in a total
vacuum of self-understanding.

In one sense, concepts of Christ have been idealizations
of human self-understanding in any period and therefore
goals for human striving. It is impossible to discover just
how much other cultural factors have influenced men's
understanding of Jesus Christ and how much he has in-

fluenced their self-understanding; how much cultural ideals have been projected on to him and how much he has shaped those ideals himself. Certainly ever since the work of David Friedrich Strauss in the last century, the view that the early Christian community crystallized its apocalyptic messianic hopes around the impressive but exclusively human figure of Jesus has been one viable approach to New Testament interpretation. But the mutual influence of a concept of Jesus and a cultural ideal of man can be seen at successive points in the history of the church: the divine logos when man's essence was thought to be reason; the man of sorrows when the utter disparity of this world and that to come was stressed in the Middle Ages; the joyous pauper of Galilee when the Franciscan ideal gripped the imagination of Europe in the face of its own struggle to reorganize its financial structure; the proclaimer of man's rational duty when a way was sought out of the chaos of religious fanaticism; the man of deep feeling and love when romanticism spoke for man's sense of final reality; and now the one free for others, the iconoclast in a day of collapsing ideologies. Does the figure of Christ now simply stampede men with the trend of the times or has he his own call and way? That is one of the current questions even with those who, regardless of the direction of modern thought and practice, find in him their ideal.

Others see the radical assertion of Jesus' historicity (which for them is the meaning of affirming his true humanity) as a denial of *his* significance for us today. Kierkegaard says at one point that it would have been enough for the apostolic generation simply to have written that God had come among them as a man.[21] Bultmann has written, "I do indeed think that we can now know almost nothing concerning the life and personality of Jesus, since the early Christian sources show no interest in either, are moreover fragmentary and often legendary; and other sources about Jesus do not exist."[22] Because Jesus is a man of the first century, we can extract only the most general fact of his obedience and faithfulness from the specific acts expressing that obedience. The only requisite "imitation of Christ" that is called for is radical obedience, but not conformity in any way to the specific patterns in which his own obedience or that of his immediate disciples found expression. To mold one's own discipleship by those patterns is simply another way of substituting a way of the world for the faith which Christ demands and is as faithless as ignoring his call.[23]

Some have understood the divine pole of Christology to be only superlatives in the human description of Jesus. To say, "Jesus is the Son of God" is, for many people, equivalent to saying, "I think more of Jesus than of any other man." *Divine* then means "I most heartily approve of." Thus, Jesus himself as a personality, his way of life, or the bare outline of his obedience to authentic existence are stamped with human approval by such use of *divine*. Any ongoing purpose of God's redemption is dissolved in a "way of speaking" about a wide range of human experiences for many people today. But to make valid comparisons at this point is exceedingly difficult just because one can get to the reference of the words only through the words.

THE QUESTION OF THE BIBLE

The Protestant is likely to meet the questions concerning God and Christ within the question of the Bible, for he claims the Bible to be the source of all true doctrine. Although it has always been known that the Bible required interpretation—the Old Testament in the light of the New, for example—the Scriptures were a recognized authority for both faith and practice, a "sufficient rule," as confessions frequently stated it. The views which were developed by scholars in the nineteenth century, but which were understood by the average Christian only in the twentieth, so emphasized the historicity of Scripture as to question its abiding authority. In our day the discussion waging on even a popular level about "demythologization" is but one example of this development.

While the whole history of Biblical interpretation is far too large for summary here (indeed, one whole volume of this series is devoted to the contemporary problem of hermeneutics), a review of certain important transitions in its course is necessary for an understanding of the present situation. In most of the theology of the Western church up to the time of the Reformation it was assumed that the Bible contained the oracles of God, albeit in various types of literature. The interpretation of this literature was held to belong to those who spoke for the community to which Scripture had been given. Thus, while any person might be able to secure a copy of the Scriptures and read them himself, he would not *rightly* understand them unless he shared in the faith of those who wrote them and those for whom they were written. For the medieval church this meant only those who were properly trained and oriented —namely, the hierarchy centering in the pope himself.

But can one know, apart from the assertions of the representatives of the community, that the Scriptures speak from beyond the authority of the human community itself; that is, that there is a Word of God in them as well as words of men? By the time of Thomas Aquinas it was argued that the dominican and apostolic miracles, the ful-

fillment of Old Testament prophecy in the New, the antiquity of the writings, and their lofty moral and spiritual
character establish them as the Word of God. The importance of these points can be seen, it was held, even by those
who do not share the Christian faith. John Calvin, however, relegated such arguments for the divine origin of
Scripture to a subordinate place, insisting that the same
Spirit who inspired their writers had also to inspire their
readers in order that the full impact of *God's* Word might
reach Christian believers of a later day. This "inner testimony of the Holy Spirit" confirmed the word of Scripture
and sealed it on the heart of the believer.

In the struggles of the pluralistic religious scene following the Reformation the attempt was made to achieve a
universal justification for Scripture, since not all could
honestly testify to the Spirit's inner witness, and not only
a universal justification of Scripture but a single universal
interpretation as well. This was an inevitable outcome of
the move of the Reformers to bypass what they considered
the distorting and false tradition of the medieval church in
order to get back to sound teaching. But while the immediate irritation was with the late nominalistic theologians,
they also felt free to go behind the tradition represented
by the "Fathers," which led to the sixteenth-century de-
bacle, to the Bible itself.

The tools for doing this were those of Renaissance hu-
manistic scholarship in general—such as textual and ancient language studies. Although the Reformers held that
the Scriptures were given to faith, it was not difficult to
make the transition to the assumption that any man with
the scholar's tools could discern the true meaning of the
Scriptures and that the various confessional traditions
could only hamper their true exegesis. This was the con-

tribution of the Socinians, who tried to make both the *teaching* and the *authority* of the Bible available to the man of reason who was seeking the true way of salvation. But in order to do this, they had to simplify the argument, basing it on some "self-evident" truth that the ordinary man could readily understand. In this way, faith could be a genuinely human possibility and decision, rather than the inexplicable working out of divine (and arbitrary) election. Any rational man, at least in the view of this position, could appreciate both the miraculous authentication of the teaching and its superlative quality—were the evidence pointed out to him for his consideration.

But this made it imperative to demonstrate the trustworthiness of the Biblical narratives and it ordained the historians and Biblical scholars as the new high priests of Christendom. For example, if the truth of Christ's teaching is manifested by his miracles, then one must verify the whole chain of transmission of the evidence of the miraculous event itself to the present day: the reliability of the witness, his ability to recognize a miracle as against the natural course of events, his faithful testimony, the accuracy of the scribe who recorded it, the faithful copying, preservation, and translation of the documents, and so forth. All this had to be established beyond a doubt to sustain the authority of the Bible as a sufficient rule both of faith and of practice.

What began with the most pious of intentions soon came to have questionable (some would say disastrous) results. In the connection between this specific question and the development of "secular" methods of historical study a new perspective obtained which threatened the miracle argument at key points. The textual problems over the centuries were minor compared with the fact that it

was increasingly recognized that the New Testament narratives simply could not support the weight that was placed
upon them by this method of seeking to substantiate their
divine authority. What man would believe a report of a
contemporary miracle if it were supported by no more
concrete evidence than is offered in the Gospels for a specific occurrence? it was asked. Further, the Bible at many
points merely reflects the cultural views of the ancient
world in general and does not provide a divinely given
and therefore unique understanding of reality.

But by far the most devastating blow was the recognition that men and cultures are inseparably related to history. At first this recognition was used to discredit the
Deists, who put forward a "religion of reason" possessed
by Adam and republished for the masses by Moses and
Jesus. Reason, it was pointed out, can tell us whether
something is true or not but in itself does not give us the
content of all truth which we must learn piecemeal in our
interaction with the world and other men. Thus, miracle
can call our attention to teaching of which we had been
unaware, reason can tell us whether or not it is true, but
again, only miracle can establish its *divine* authority.
Later, the historical perspective was turned against the
argument from miracle itself by showing that the argument's efficacy depended upon a particular cultural mind-
set of those with whom it was to be used. And, as history
amply showed, men did not always think that way.

In that Paul did not write like John and that the Old
Testament reflected the ways of ancient Israel as against
the Greco-Roman world of the first century, Christians
were long aware of the human element in Scripture. But
at the beginning of the nineteenth century, it was questioned whether God "spoke through" these various forms
of expression with his own authentic word, accommodat-

ing himself, as Calvin put it, to man's understanding; or whether the Scriptures were only human attempts to express a thoroughly human meaning that had certain divine overtones. Schleiermacher, for example, replaced the view of divine dictation with the picture of a religious community, drawn together by spontaneous outpourings of religious feeling, expressing itself in dance, ritual, liturgy, and finally in literature. With him the corner has been turned. From then on, any Biblical statement would be set against the man who wrote it and within his environment, not against the unchangeable background of eternity. This new historical perspective would whisper, even though the question was not always heard, "Why absolutize the first century?" Instead of "Here is the Word of God," there would be, "This is the way Paul thought about it." And with a world so radically changed as ours is compared to the first century, it is not surprising that even convinced Christians began to wonder about the authority of Paul's words for men today.

Still, the antithesis was drawn between Jesus and his interpreters, implying that somehow he was unaffected by this solvent of historical relativity. But it quickly reached him too. First there was the recognition that much of the New Testament material is not historical or biographical but kerygmatic, i.e., its concern is to express faith or to bring men to faith, not to convey ordinary knowledge about Jesus as a man. Strauss insisted that much in the New Testament was *myth*—by which he meant philosophical truth set in the form of a historical narrative. For this reason, the narrative could not be taken at face value as giving us facts about the life of Jesus. Instead of a simple picture of Jesus and his teaching, the Gospels present us with a very complex phenomenon. Strauss saw the key to the puzzle in the early church's focusing its own messianic hopes on the enigmatic figure of Jesus of Nazareth. His teacher F. C. Baur found in the New Testament the polemics of the universalist (Pauline) or the narrower (Petrine) parties or attempts to reconcile the conflict between the two. Wellhausen had arranged the Old Testament in an evolutionary order, insisting that monotheism could not have been Israel's faith during the Mosaic period but was instead a postexilic development. While many people were outwardly unaffected by these scholarly efforts, it was evident even in the resolute attempt to maintain the older view of the Bible that the answer to the question no longer could be taken for granted.

Yet just with these developments the hope burned that the methods of modern historiography could get behind the faith evaluations to the real man, and it was assumed that in contact with the historical Jesus, as against the first or second century Christ of faith, today's men could make their own response to him, a more valid response at that because of their superior knowledge and human understanding. Such an assumption is a strange mixture of respect and contempt for history. On the one hand, it involves the knowledge that all human forms are historical and therefore not ultimate. No one, not even a disciple of the circle of twelve, can escape history. But on the other hand, there is an unjustified conceit that somehow contemporary forms avoid past mistakes and hence are more true than those of the past. Somehow this assumes that men can negate the past to go beyond the past and hence find some essence or meaning distinct from historical forms.

So long as the effort was directed toward finding the *real* Jesus, as against the assumed distortions in the early church's witness concerning him, there was little problem for faith. For faith was committed to *him* as Lord, not to some historical conception of him, and to know *him* would make faith more informed if not more valid. The attempt to uncover his humanity, however, soon imprisoned him within the first century. The nineteenth century wrestled with its kenotic Christologies, now frequently understood as the *total* outpouring of God's transcendence into humanity, so that the ongoing course of mankind itself rather than the single person of Jesus of Nazareth is taken as the locus of the incarnation. In affirming the radical historicity of Jesus, the total relativity of his teaching is also affirmed, and this sets a tremendous problem for those who are serious about the *Christian* life.

The problem manifests itself at several levels. For example, although they held that the total Bible was God's Word, most traditional Christians felt no compulsion to take the Mosaic legislation seriously. The Ten Commandments were distilled from the rest of the Law, but Christian communities felt no obligation to follow the Biblical provisions for determining guilt when a man was discovered to have been murdered outside a town. A higher level of the problem is met in the case of the demonology of the Gospels. By and large, people now are inclined to say that Jesus' belief in demons simply reflects his citizenship in the first century and does not give divine sanction to this cosmology. Some would say that demonology is only the framework in which the human evangelists cast the story. Others would say that the divine-human Jesus merely accommodated himself to the prevailing beliefs of the people in order that he might be understood. At any rate, in various ways we find justification in dropping demonology, even when we seek to penetrate its form for the truth it contains.

But is it so easy to say that Jesus' prayer life and his instruction in prayer are also only a passing form of the first century? Did Jesus pray only because first century man

(of which he was one example) thought that a supernatural world stood above this world and aid from it
could be summoned in crises? And can we therefore, in
contradistinction to Jesus, as Paul van Buren suggests, regard prayer as self-contained meditation on how we might
help people who fall within our concern?[24]

Or perhaps for many who have already adopted this
"secular" view of prayer, the question could be faced on a
still more troublesome level in what they take to be his
teaching and acting in freedom for others, in laying foundations for our understanding of human brotherhood and
the like. Perhaps these forms, too, although we find them
more acceptable today, are just as historically conditioned
as New Testament demonology. And in this case we are
faced with the really radical question, "Why bother with
Scripture at all, whether it be Paul's advice about the dress
of Corinthian women or Jesus' admonition to take no
thought for the morrow, much less the dietary laws of
Leviticus?" It seems as though we have our own wisdom
derived from our own sources and that we find sympathetic
echoes of that wisdom in parts of Scripture. Is it so clear
that our criteria of wisdom or our pattern of action are
drawn *from* Scripture?

Even before the midpoint of the nineteenth century,
Kierkegaard pointed to the problem of how one might
establish a contemporaneity with Jesus in a way that did not
get lost in the endless footnote of historical investigation
and critical study. The function of Scripture is not to give
us knowledge of Jesus and his disciples as men, but to con-
front us with the decision of faith which is ours to make.
This faith, moreover, is not defined by its content in a
dogmatic sense but by its form. As Gerhard Ebeling puts
it, "The Christian faith is not a special faith, but faith

pure and simple." Christian faith is true faith just as Christian love is not a special sort of love but genuine, real love.[25]

The emphasis must therefore be placed on the preaching and the hearing of Scripture in its relation to contemporary human decision. The choice is set before men: authentic or inauthentic existence, which means life in the full realization of the unique freedom that can be man's, or life as simply a reaction to or acquiescence with pressures and forces which surround man. The New Testament issues the call to freedom. But the use of this freedom, or rather the expression of this freedom, must take forms strictly relevant to our own age, not imitated from an earlier period. Bultmann calls specific attention to the Biblical cosmology of the three-storied universe with earth midway between heaven and hell and insists that it can no longer be taken at face value in our world which denies the sort of supernatural interaction that the older view affirmed.

But the presupposition that the human existential situation remains the same throughout the ages and that this forms our bond to the men of the New Testament church is precisely what is to be questioned. It is simply another manifestation of the metaphysical principle that essence precedes existence. The existential situation of a man living in a universe controlled by God who responds to the prayers and supplications of his worshipers is not the same as the existential situation of a man who sees himself "thrown" into existence. As Jean-Paul Sartre said in his classic lecture on existentialism and humanism, it makes a profound difference if God is not. Everything is changed. And everything is permitted.[26] The current renewed interest in the historical Jesus, which seeks to use the faith statements about him rather than exclude them on principle, witnesses to the final unsatisfactoriness of the existential answer to the Biblical problem. There can be no question, however, but that this approach opened the eyes of many people to dimensions of truth in the Bible that they had never suspected were there and made the Bible of contemporary rather than of antiquarian interest.

For this view, the attempt to get back to an authoritative "Word of God" is likely to be taken as but another example of the flight from personal responsibility—from a radical "Here I stand," in which one's own decision is clearly expressed, to "The Bible says," in which one attempts to lose himself in a universal law for which God is responsible, thus avoiding the radical personal decision of faith. Ever since the days of Luther and Calvin debate has waged over the question of the "third use of the law." Lutherans and Calvinists agreed that the law serves to uncover sin and regulate the lives of unbelievers (and the lives of Christians too, insofar as they remain unbelievers). But the Calvinists insisted that the law does this only by setting forth God's will which is not found in man's knowledge as man. Thus the law has a third function—guiding the believer, who sincerely loves God and seeks his will, in his Christian life. In this framework, Christians are saved from the *curse* of the law and from servile bondage to the law (in the sense that the law is set over against what a man himself really wants), but the law in the new relationship of faith now shows ignorant but teachable men what God would have them do and what the love of Christ means within the human, historical situation.

The contemporary form of this issue is the question as to whether there is a *word* to be set over against a hermeneutic of that word. For many, and this seems true of

Ebeling, the whole reality is subsumed under hermeneutic itself, for a word over against our decision to hear a word would be but another form of law. If Scripture does not engage us by canceling our own structures of understanding, then we must assume responsibility for what it says. It speaks to us, as it were, our own deepest insights. In much contemporary theology it is not clear whether God speaks *through* the deepest human insight or *to* it. Hence, on one side of this issue are ranged the various types of immanentist thought all the way from those which regard "God" as only another way of speaking of certain aspects of *human* existence to those which speak quasi-historically of God "pouring himself" completely into this world in man. And on the other side are ranged those views which emphasize the qualitative difference (albeit within a context of communion) between God and man and see men's finest insights and noblest aspirations over against God's truth and righteousness. So it would seem that Gabriel Vahanian, for example, would argue.[27]

Many lament this indecisiveness of the current theological scene, and many, not understanding the issues involved, will call for a return to the "simple faith" of the past. But the past only appears simple in retrospect because the debates which then raged have been forgotten and only safe conclusions remembered, or because mass communication brings the theological debate to the conscious level of everyman, whereas before most church members were unaware not only of the debate but of the relatively secure results of scholarship which almost a century later appear radical to many. In that respect it is pitiful that only now are people becoming aware of the issues fought over in the last hundred years.

But it is the concerns which are the subjects of the present discussion which put the Christian life in a different context from the days when men could assume that God had spoken in Scripture to give them the clear plan for a way of life leading to sure salvation. In view of the recognition of historical relativity as it encompasses Bible and traditional theology, what does the *Christian* life mean? Has it any characteristic or style of its own?

CHAPTER III

The World Come of Age

It would be easy, in the face of the uncertainty we have
mentioned and particularly in relation to the challenge to
traditional ways of understanding Christian faith and life,
to regard the developments of Western culture since the
Renaissance as the great apostasy of which we are warned
in the Gospels (Matt. 24:12). Men seem to be drawing their
inspiration from the world, not from God. They question
the words and commands of Jesus Christ even while they
profess to obey him. They find no place for God whose
sons they claim to be. They propose to carry on a mission
by denying the very reason for the mission. Against this
sort of challenge what can the real Christian do but call
for a return to true faith, to a world where "God" means
something, to a discipleship that can be recognized by its
continuity with that of faithful Christians throughout the
ages?

For those who rate the status of religion or Christianity
by the condition of the institutional church this is especially true. Haven't the Supreme Court decisions, putting
an end to a long-cherished "Christian" atmosphere in the
schools, declared the state to be against the church no
matter how inoffensively nonsectarian it might be in ex-

pressing itself? Isn't the incorporation of Sunday into the regular routine of work and play an outright denial that man's life is set against eternity and that he needs more than bread alone in order to live? And isn't the present questioning of the churches' tax-exempt status a repudiation of their contributions to the welfare and stability of society? Hasn't the prestige of the minister—the "man of God"—dropped below that of the other professions instead of capping them as the "first citizen" of the community? How can Christians look at all this other than as a slip, a fall, a denial of all that the church believes and seeks to do?

There is great danger that the whole modern phenomenon might be evaluated from such a parochial stance that its significance and opportunities are hopelessly distorted. Any responsible person, particularly the Christian, must balance a concern to preserve the meanings and values of the past with an openness to change and new possibilities. But it is not easy to recognize that new possibilities at times mean a radical reorientation in which everything must be thought through again. Yet if one can step back from the immediate moment, he may begin to see the extensive dimensions of what has been happening in and to human thought in the last century and a half.

Epochs of Human Thought

Cornelis A. van Peursen, of the University of Leiden, outlines three periods of human history involving three ways of thinking, three "approaches to reality"—although it would be wrong to see these in a strictly chronological sequence.[1] The structure of his analysis is certainly not new in Western thought, however. Auguste Comte, the nineteenth-century originator of sociology, spoke of the theological, metaphysical, and positivistic stages of human thought. And he had before him such threefold patterns as Giambattista Vico's ages of gods, heroes, and men, or Joachim de Fiore's ages of the Father, Son, and Holy Spirit.

In the theological stage of Comte's analysis, everything is accounted for in terms of supernatural causes or forces. On the metaphysical level, things are explained in terms of a "reality" which lies "underneath" or "beyond" sensible reality. But in the positivistic stage, descriptive laws of natural behavior are scientifically derived, by which men are enabled to predict the course of nature and control it. Comte looked forward to the day when the methods of natural science could be applied to the study of man, producing a "scientific" moral guidance. Later in his life, he even tried to develop a religion of humanity in which a clergy scientifically trained and oriented would shape the life of the community.

In a similar threefold fashion, van Peursen describes first the *mythical* period in which the distinction between the natural and the human has not been drawn. Nature is understood in human (personalized) terms and man in natural terms. The concern in this period is *that* something is—in other words, with *cosmogony*. Such a frame of thought, dominated by divine forces, produces the medicine-man controlled society. The concern with *origin* prevents the development of real history. (One of the important meanings of Professor Altizer's use of the phrase "death of God" as an event in history is that God's "death" is the event which makes all history possible.)

The stage that Comte spoke of as metaphysical, van Peursen calls the period of *ontology*. Here the deliverance from magic is brought about by the withdrawing of the divine forces to their own abode, thereby creating the two separate realms of the sacred and the profane. Man is now distinguished from nature or the cosmos. The question is not cosmogony in this period but *cosmology, what something is*. Reason becomes the agent of mastering the universe—but reason in the sense of explaining and accounting for. In this stage of thought, society is divided up into a plurality of distinct kingdoms. But the danger in the ontological stage is to think of isolated substances as entities in themselves—the *Ding-an-sich,* to use Kant's term.

The third period, which Comte called positivistic, van Peursen characterizes as the *functional*. Functional thinking departs from the ontological ideal to serve as a tool in human society. The concern to build a structure of pure thought mirroring the world gives way to the use of thought to change the world. Only that to which men are directly related is regarded as real. "The nouns of the ontological era become the verbs of the functional era," he writes.[2] Ethical values, for example, instead of being metaphysical realities are ways of organizing human society. The question of God must now be discussed around the theme of what function he serves. And the world is dealt with as one huge organization run by men. The danger here is "operational thinking," which means that reality is identified with operations of the human mind; and men too lose themselves in operations.

What van Peursen discusses is relevant not only to religion but to the sciences and ethics as well. The concept of "cause" in physics has changed radically from the metaphysics of "legal agent" in Aristotle's thinking. Although any particular man today may actually move from one of these epochs to another, the problem which Christians face is whether their message has any meaning and relevance in the functional era, or whether they can speak only to men by calling them back to the ontological or mythical periods.

Harvey Cox has called attention to another dimension of the problem in reviewing the suggestions of Marshall McLuhan concerning "post-literate" man. McLuhan notes that the transition from the mythical stage of human thought to the metaphysical is concurrent with the development of writing. The age of writing forced men, so to speak, to adopt a linear perspective that affected religious and social thought: "The linear sense of time is part of the metaphysics of books and print."[3] Now with motion pictures, television, computers, and the like, the age of writing may be past—not in the sense that books will no longer be written and read, but in the sense that men's views of life and the world will make an epochal change. Corporate forms are likely to replace individual ones associated with reading and reflecting on a book. Even church life, Cox says, will shift in emphasis: "The visible *style* of the church's life will become a much more significant element in the communication of the gospel."[4]

This changing perspective of all thought and conceptualization lies at the root of the demand for new ways of thinking about the Christian theology mentioned in the last chapter. The creeds and confessions of traditional Christian faith have come, by and large, from the period of ontological thinking. The Bible comes from perhaps the even earlier mythological period. The danger may lie in thinking that to participate in the move to functional thought is to fall away from Christian truth.

BIBLICAL FAITH AND THE DEATH OF THE GODS

On the contrary, a good case can be made for the thesis that Christianity has been one of the major forces making

for this development and that the modern secular age is
its creation. But this observation in no way minimizes the
difficulties faced by Christians. "If, in the period of mythical sensitiveness, faith could find its expression through
the dynamic word of the prophets and apostles, if it could
respond to Greek ontologism by an equally metaphysical
theology, it hardly seems able to find as easy an answer at
the present time to the secularization of the modern
world," writes Amedeo Molnar of the Comenius Theological Faculty in Prague. "In contrast to the preceding
periods, the man of today is 'inoculated' against any re-
lapse into the Christian faith which is viewed as a regret-
table illness."[5]

Harvey Cox, who gives the most readily understandable
presentation of this view that Christian faith has shaped
the modern age and ought not flee from it, says that the
world was desacralized as the result of the revelation of
the God of the Bible. The doctrine of creation, which
has a unique significance in the Bible, makes God something other than the world so that the realm of nature
cannot be regarded as sacred or divine in its own right.[6]
As Gabriel Vahanian has put it, "The world is not divine
but is the theater of God's glory."[7] Further, the events of
the exodus of Israel from Egypt and the subsequent wilderness wanderings destroyed the sacredness of politics by
making God's will something other than the maintenance
of the *status quo*. Finally, the whole realm of human
values was desacralized in the Sinai command forbidding
any representation of God. Since nothing taken from the
world can represent (stand for) God, nothing dare become
that for which everything else is to be sacrificed.

All this means that men are given *this* world as the context of their lives, a world whose "meaning" finally derives

from the meaning they give it, a world which is amenable to their control and for which they bear full responsibility. In this world there is no sacred "religious" province because the sacred belongs to God alone who is not of this world. No one aspect or collection of aspects of this world can be treated with religious awe. All is open to man for his use. Or as Cox graphically puts it, "A highly disparate conglomerate of value systems can co-exist in a society so long as they all repudiate the privilege of winning the others over by rack and thumbscrew."[8] The task of the community of faith, proclaiming the God who has thus desacralized nature, politics, and ethics, is to call men to maturity out of the ages of mythology and ontology.

In fact, giving any part of the world ultimate significance is idolatry. Idolatry is faithlessness to God manifested in setting up something which is not God in his place. Cox suggests that such idolatry evident in the failure to recognize the God of universal concern, along with technical inadequacy, has prevented man's full transition from tribal and town cultures to the city. The tribe, for example, belongs to the mythological stage of religion. In the development of town culture, tribal deities must be subordinated to a god who can represent the whole community. But the shift from town to urban culture requires a God great enough to relativize all previous loyalties. The "common ancestor" doctrine stood in the way of the growth of Athens or Rome into genuine cities. Urbanization, then, is the context of desacralization in which local traditions disintegrate to be replaced by functional relationships. In the true city, the question of whether a man is a Jew, Italian, or old-line American is unimportant in relation to his performing needed services or using those which are available.

It is not clear, however, from what Cox says, whether the social change precipitates the religious change (an enlarged concept of God) or whether it waits for such a God to be revealed. Later, in his adaptation of classical two-natures Christology in his view of the Kingdom of God as both a man-made and divine gift, this problem is taken up again.[9] Idolatry is a perennial problem, and even today in the age of technopolis it leads to a retreat to town or tribal mentality, often on a national scale.

Thomas J. J. Altizer speaks to this point when he says that the real freedom of man is bound up with his hearing the gospel. Far from being at the mercy of the changing forms of life and thought, Christianity has, in effect, announced them beforehand and has brought them about. Both words and concepts are slippery, and it is misleading to establish ties between men on the basis of the mere words that they use. Cox specifically repudiates "God is dead" language although he recognizes that the word "God" must take on new meanings today.[10] Yet there is an important relationship between what Altizer is talking about and the secular city which Cox sees as the unique context of contemporary Christian life. Altizer, like Cox, inveighs against any religion (or ideology) which would call men out of the present age back into the ages of myth or metaphysics. Such an appeal would deny the God who has led us into our own age. A god of primal beginnings and even a metaphysical God as "First Cause" is dead. These are not living options for us today, according to Altizer.

He reverts to mythical language, however, when he speaks of God's willing his own annihilation. "God has willed" that he no longer be known in the old ways—either in the primitive immediacy of the age of myth or the reflection of the age of metaphysics. "We must recognize that the proclamation of the death of God is a Christian confession of faith."[11] "The radical Christian proclaims that God has actually died in Christ, that this death is both a historical and a cosmic event, and, as such, it is a final and irrevocable event, which cannot be reversed by a subsequent religious or cosmic movement."[12] The incarnation means—again in mythical language—that God wills now to be known in and through the history of *this* world. Thus, the abandonment of traditional forms is not apostasy. Rather, the attempt to resurrect and refurbish them is apostasy, unfaithfulness to God who does not call us into the past but into the future. Failure to recognize this turns God into Satan, man's enemy. "Rather than being mute and numb in response to the advent of a world in which the original name of God is no longer sayable, the Christian can live and speak by pronouncing the word of God's death, by joyously announcing the 'good news' of the death of God, and by greeting the naked reality of our experience as the triumphant realization of the self-negation of God. What can the Christian fear of the power of darkness when he can name our darkness as the fulfillment of the self-emptying of God in Christ?"[13]

It would be wrong to suggest that there are no dangers of radical infidelity to Christian faith in such a transition. Emphasis on the "gradual and progressive metamorphosis of Spirit into flesh"[14] can conceivably lead to the false religion of secularism which Cox sets against the authentic movement of secularization (or desacralization in Vahanian's thought). At times it seems as though the course of history for Altizer can never go wrong in such a way that it cannot correct its own mistakes. And yet he also stresses the risk in the movement that he calls for: "To refuse a deity who is a sovereign and alien other, or to will the death of the transcendent Lord, is certainly to risk an ultimate wrath and judgment, a judgment which Christianity has long proclaimed to be damnation. . . . No honest contemporary seeker can ever lose sight of the very real possibility that the willing of the death of God is the way to madness, dehumanization, and even to the most totalitarian form of society yet realized in history."[15] On the other hand, it is the only way to the new humanity in Christ. But to refuse the risk is really to wager on the "religious" Christ and to forfeit the actuality of time and history.[16]

Risk or no, the positive contribution of Christian faith to the modern secular world is important. According to Dr. Arend Th. van Leeuwen, the secularity of Western civilization carries Christianity along with it so that Christian concern must be expressed through participation in the forward movement of Christian history. It is this movement which has produced the secularism that has broken the control of religions all over the world. Any future the church now has must lie beyond, not behind, the secular revolution.[17]

William Hamilton emphasizes that secularization marks a release to be celebrated rather than a loss to be mourned. In *The New Essence of Christianity*, first published in 1961, he spoke of contemporary Christians being "reduced to fragments, partial vision, broken speech, not because of the unbelieving world 'out there,' but precisely because that unbelieving world has come to rest within ourselves."[18] In other words, the phenomenon producing the agony of theology was essentially unbelief. It was due to the growing sense "that God has withdrawn, that he is absent, even that he is somehow dead."[19] "Little wonder that

Lent is the only season when we are at home, and that that cry of dereliction from the cross is sometimes the only biblical word that can speak to us."[20] In discussing the "style" of the Christian's life, Hamilton in the same book stressed resignation as against the traditional Calvinist rebellion against the *status quo* in the interest of a *Christian* world.[21] We are enabled thereby not only to suffer with the world but also to enjoy it. And if this seems insufficient for the future, he wrote, it is enough for today in which alone we are asked "to think, to live, and to obey God."[22]

In his writings five years later, Hamilton emphasizes the element of enjoyment. Radical theology, he says, is optimistic, relating itself to the "hope and optimism of American life today, a conviction that substantive changes in the lives of men can and will be made."[23] "We shall overcome" is today's mood and it ought not to be disparaged. In another article, entitled "The New Optimism—from Prufrock to Ringo," this theme of *celebrating* the absence of God is developed further.[24] The demise of neo-orthodoxy, he says, was the result of its abandoning politics in the '50s for existentialist philosophy. But there is no further need for caution against *possessing* God, since now he is absent, and in this absence there is place for the rejoicing of purposeless play—hence the sheer exuberance of Ringo and his brother Beatles. Without God, there is no tragedy to sap human attention. Experiencing God makes man lose sight of the world. Modern man wagers on man, not on God as Pascal did. Conditions creating despair can be overcome. Our task lies along that road rather than in speaking of a hope beyond despair, an optimism of grace alone.

Although there is a betraying stridency in these words about rejoicing in God's absence that does not characterize Cox's writings, the hope for the future is clear—a hope that is made possible by man's being freed from irrelevant religious claims to put his technology and science to work solving human problems. But this can happen only as the world is desacralized in one area after another, as the gods —or their twentieth-century counterparts—are deposed. Just as taboos in the lives of primitive people hamper the ministrations of doctors and teachers intent on helping them, so our refined taboos of the "sacred" provinces of life stand in the way of our progress. But just as primitive man may seem to prefer his old animistic ways, so many in our time are deeply disturbed and unsettled by the secularization of the sacred.

CONTEMPORARY ICONOCLASM

The very existence of the metropolis depends upon the process of desacralization bringing the world totally within man's control. In this sense, one can say that "nothing is sacred" is the principle of modern urban existence. Forests, which many would preserve from a sense of wonder at nature, are quickly bulldozed away and burned to clear ground for an expressway or housing project. Characteristic neighborhoods with their equivalent of "Old World charm" are broken up in the course of urban renewal. Ancient landmarks are removed to smooth the flow of traffic. Gems of architecture of an earlier generation crumble before the wreckers. As Maxwell Anderson put it in *High Tor,* "Nothing is made by man but makes, in the end, good ruins." Only now even the ruins are obliterated.

So also the anonymity and mobility which belong to men in the metropolis are the result of eliminating traditional but unwanted distracting close relationships characteristic of town life. Instead of being bound to a situation by insurmountable pressures—either physical realities or quasi-religious forces—men are free to move to points of opportunity and fulfillment. Cox likens this deliverance from unwanted restrictions to the freedom of the gospel as against the law which exerts external control over men.[25]

Secularization delivers thinking from the shackles of "orthodoxies" of various types, particularly from thought as an end in itself so that it can tackle the practical problems of the day. Whereas Paul Tillich spoke of religion as having to do with ultimate and therefore essentially metaphysical questions and found these questions inescapably asked by men on every hand,[26] Cox holds that man is freed from the burden of such ultimate questions in order that he might deal realistically with what Bonhoeffer called the "penultimate" questions concerning human life in this world, leaving in God's hands the ultimate issues. To import God's concerns into this world is simply to create the sacred as a special province.[27]

Desacralization as thus far described, however, could be confused with heedlessness. Much of what goes on in urban and national life can be attributed to a loss of the sense of obligation to future generations as well as of responsibility to those past. Under the demands of an immediate situation action may be taken to relieve the pressure of a problem with little thought for long-term consequences. The mushrooming of housing developments with their fantastic squandering of the resource of land and their lack of adequate transportation arrangements is but one example. But on the other hand, uncritical commitment to certain ideals and programs, especially when these are dignified by religious significance, prevents men from coming to terms with present reality. The obvious example is the identification of "Christian" and "individualist" which sets many churchmen against social programs trying to wrestle

with the realities of mass social pressures. Commitments
of this sort frequently lead to distorted views of the world
simply because the true facts no longer justify them and
their support must come from distortions of reality.

But what does the desacralization of the world mean?
Take the question of political systems as an example. The
historical role of Christian groups in the struggle for modern representative government is well known, although it
was not the sole source of agitation for "free government."
The ancient world knew republics and democracies, but
always with a severely limited enfranchisement. There is
no question but that many who fought, worked, and
planned for establishing modern Western democracies felt
that this form of government could best express and guar-
antee the status of men understood as God's children and
heirs to his Kingdom. But having said all this, it is quite
another matter to say that democracy is the *Christian* form
of government and that Christians are bound to further
its extension as one aspect of their divine mandate in the
world.

It is entirely possible, in view of the cultural and economic situations of many of the world's peoples today, that
other forms of government can best accomplish the purpose of government: to provide the opportunity for a full
life for all. Christians for the most part have already made
this adjustment in regard to church government, where a
variety of patterns are mutually respected, from congregational democracy to monarchial episcopacy. Yet in in-
ternational affairs they frequently swing from a naïve
insistence on "free elections" to a cynical accommodation
to tyrannical power structures. In the face of this problem,
Karl Barth, following the example of Jeremiah's advice to
the Babylonian exiles, encouraged Christians in commu-

nist lands to take up their lives within the communist structures rather than lay hopes on revolution directed toward the patterns of Western governments.[28] The very branding of communist states as "unchristian" has prevented people in the West from being at all sympathetic with those who see communism as a sound political course in today's world. And it has kept entirely out of mind Christians of the East who have regarded communist revolutions of the Western proletariate as the first step toward a genuinely Christian economic order.

As acknowledged religious loyalties wane, emotional commitments are transferred rather than eliminated. Today very few would take up arms in the Protestant-Catholic dispute as Europe did in the Thirty Years' War, but they will fight on other issues which they regard as ultimate. So today the watchword is not so likely to be a particular form of institutional religion as "freedom" for the "American way of life." But in less sweeping perspectives, the label and emotional significance of "Christian" is apt to be applied to a particular course of action. For example, integration of schools is held by many to be a "Christian" position as against "unchristian segregation." Less certain for most is what the "Christian" stand should be in regard to birth control, especially outside the dimensions of responsible family planning.

In the early church and the medieval church, battles raged over the use of pictures and images as aids to devotion. The question was, Is there a legitimate use of them to represent God in the world? But the problem lies much deeper than the type of art used to decorate churches. The question is whether the "ultimate" can be "used" to reinforce what otherwise would be purely human values. Once employed, it provokes an uncritical attachment to a course of action which ought to be subjected to the closest scrutiny. To use again the example of school integration, if integration is "Christian," then any step toward it must be supported as a "Christian" move, even though a host of other considerations might be involved. In many cities it is now proposed to transport children from one district to another in order that schools can have a more equal proportion of racial groups. The values of integation in this case must be set against the disvalue of forcing small children into a plurality of communities—the home, neighborhood, school, church, etc.—all different. But for those who have already decided that integration is "Christian," to raise these other questions is itself "unchristian." "Christian" in such a frame of reference takes on *religious* overtones and sacralizes the profane.

Here a difference later to be explored must be noted: while Reinhold Niebuhr concerned himself with "Christian" positions on contemporary political and social issues, Karl Barth is most suspicious of any attempt to make God a party to some provisional human program. The plea that Harvey Cox and others make for contemporary iconoclasm is a repudiation of the aura of "Christian" in order that issues can be examined and dealt with in terms of genuine possibilities. Iconoclasm today is thus a plea for a greater measure of objectivity because religion is too often associated with uncritical support or rejection. Considerable thought must be given to the real meaning of "Christian" as against "sacred" or "religious" as Christians are called to responsible life in the world.

Two other representative areas can be examined from this same perspective of desacralization. The first is that of work. Not only has the Protestant concept of vocation been frequently misunderstood (as it is when it is thought to focus in specific jobs), but it has itself become an idol by making one's acceptance in society depend upon the work that he does. This marks an interesting contrast to classical culture of antiquity where leisure was the idol demanding slavery for its worship. Paul admonished those who dropped their earthly responsibilities in order to await the return of Christ with the dictum: "If any one will not work, let him not eat" (II Thess. 3:6–12). The Reformers, in protesting the elevation of the "religious" (monks and nuns) over the people engaged in day-by-day work in the world, sought to make the common life the area of true service to God. Christian faith, they held, does not call the believer out of the world but rather ever more deeply into it.

Today, however, work in its most practical and mundane dimensions has itself become a sacred object of veneration so that truly "good" persons must be engaged in work—or a reasonably exact facsimile of it. And this has meant that one who has no work—either by choice as in retirement or by social and economic contingencies such as unemployment or overage—all too often loses his status in the community. Neither he nor the community understands what role he is to fulfill. A censuring attitude may have had practical justification in times and situations when every pair of hands was desperately needed for the survival of the community. It becomes a real problem, however, now that not only power machinery but automated machinery can meet so much of human need. One economist, for example, has estimated that only two percent of the present labor force will be necessary to maintain automated production. Hence the insistence that everyone be engaged in productive work is an idolization of a particular value of the past. It has shaped attitudes toward the unemployed and the unemployable, toward families dependent upon public aid, toward the role of "senior citizens," especially in regard to the level of community support that these people are to receive. The Great Depression of the '30s showed that not everyone seeking work can always find it, but the idol that still dictates our attitudes toward the problem remains.

It may well be, of course, that one's self-respect does somehow depend psychologically upon the contribution he can make to his community—a contribution to be measured in wider ways than mundane practicality, however. For many, the question of whether a job "pays" is more important than any creative social function it may serve. Only in recent years has American life provided anything near wide acceptance for the artist, the musician, and the scholar. It may be that dimensions of this problem have not even been considered because of the more obvious economic factor of automation. The Pennsylvania Dutch way of life which binds human existence to the soil, while it makes for stability and harmony between man and nature, is not an option for large sections of the population. The "little place in the country with a few chickens" of an earlier generation's retirement dreams now seems neither feasible nor desirable.

But the point is that the whole problem should be open for investigation and discussion—thorough investigation in all dimensions, some of which may not even be apparent today—without answers being determined by uncritical commitments, by an idolatry of work.

Another typical area in which the contemporary problem of idolatry can be seen is that of sex. Attitudes toward all its phenomena are complex. On the one hand are the physiological, psychological, and sociological studies of sexual behavior that have greatly increased our knowledge of the subject—often over the protests of those who regard sex as too sacred or at least too intimately personal for such investigation. And on the other hand is the "cult" of sex to which too much modern life, from advertising to education, is subservient. For many, sex may be too sacred to study scientifically but not so sacred that it cannot be exploited to sell deodorants to younger teen-agers or soft drinks to their parents.

In spite of all the attention given to sex, little is known of its operation, particularly in its normal as against abnormal manifestations. Widespread attention and criticism was given Dr. Albert C. Kinsey's pioneering studies of sexual behavior. Recently the Johnson and Masters volume *Human Sexual Response* has renewed the debate on an even more intense level because these researchers did not depend upon what their subjects said but made direct and intricate studies of sexual orgasm, using 382 women and 312 men in an eleven-year study. The doctors supervising the research explained that frequently they and their colleagues are called on to advise patients experiencing various difficulties both personal and marital, but that they have no real foundation for their advice. Albert Rosenfeld, science editor of *Life* magazine, comments that because of the nature of the experiments, the study can be regarded as only a beginning and that it has not necessarily achieved statistically significant results. Reviewing the book, he writes:

I am old fashioned enough to share all the qualms about the propriety of employing these techniques. And I find it hard to believe that normal people can perform naturally under a set of circumstances which, it seems to me, ought to be so embarrassing and inhibiting as to render them impotent. But the testimony of researchers and subjects alike seems to refute my doubts. When all is considered, I cast my vote with Dr. Masters. It is better to know these things than not to know them.[29]

The number of those who, after voicing protests and misgivings, cast their vote with Dr. Masters is the evidence for the desacralization of sex—in this particular dimension. Many, and by no means always on presumed Christian grounds, regard the sex act itself as so intimately personal as to preclude this sort of examination. Yet the same was said in an earlier age about the dissection of cadavers and in this generation about obtaining the more intimate personal information that now is taken for granted in routine personnel questionnaires and tests. That this sort of information can be misused is patent. In the same way, the genetic information that might be used to prevent mongoloid births might conceivably be used to create a race of servile and docile workers or subjects. But if man is not simply to be at the mercy of external circumstances, then in this area also the "sacred" walls must fall to research and study.

The Last Idol

Although it was Christian teaching that freed the world from its sacred overtones so that it could be the proper object for scientific study, that study itself and the results that it achieves are not consciously ordered to the greater glory of God. Rather, they are directed to man for his own purposes. In technology, man assumes responsibility for the world and its reconstruction. But in doing so, he assumes his essential innocence; for while he will acknowledge his flaws, he assumes that he has within himself the base upon which he can plan and execute the necessary corrections.

Liberal theology often spoke of the "infinite worth of human personality," declaring all other values subordinate to this one. But in what does this worth of personality rest and what are its implications for daily life? Contemporary ethics is full of references to the value of persons as against things, but what does this mean? One could justifiably say that the various sacred orders of nature held their inviolate character only derivatively from man himself. They were extensions of his personal value. Consequently, their violation was a violation of man's own person. One by one these things have been taken out of the realm of the sacred and the personal—like peeling an onion; but the question as to what remains when they have been so reinterpreted haunts us. The aura of mystery attached to sex, for example, was largely because of its intimate personal nature. Men were not eager to expose the full details of their sex life because this was their *personal* concern. To drag it into the open was to expose the person. What then is the human value which demands that the human value of reticence make way for research? The question of knowledge for its own sake? But this too is a *human* value.

The issue is a poignant one for contemporary ethics as it turns its attention to the "human use of human beings." What is the justification for using human beings themselves in research, especially when they are unaware of their being so used? For whose benefit is the information thus obtained to be used? For mankind's? But how does mankind express its will to those who control such matters? What prevents technopolis from engaging in an even more vast Nazi "experiment"?

The facile answer is that the freedom provided by desacralization be used for the *maturity* of man. "We are freed *from* the prudential ethic, the slavery to production, the tight little family or the metaphysical jails of the past not just to revel in the new roominess of life (although reveling is clearly in order too); we are freed *for* the task of growing up."[30] But as Mr. Bloy, who gives this answer, indicates, if freedom is not to become anarchy, it must be guided by some judgment-empowering perspective. The traditional Christian church is unable to provide such a perspective, he holds, because it too often serves as the refuge for "cultural dropouts." He finds the key in Jesus "as the model of human adulthood *and* as the eschatological clue to the meaning and direction of history."[31] But church history is ample witness to the fact that nearly every cultural relativity has been read into the figure of Jesus and from that position of preeminence has been allowed to sanctify itself.

The problem is of course not new. Throughout Christian history, debate has waged concerning the *locus* of human freedom. While some have found it in man's rational nature, others have seen reason as but a more elaborate response mechanism which fulfills essentially the same function as instinct or appetite in animals. Others have located freedom in the radical nature of the will itself, but opponents have noted that a will undirected by reason may actually respond to unconscious pressures. For example, while one can say that the breakdown of family authority gives the child more freedom to choose his value systems, it may also make him more amenable to the value system of his peers, the education system, or the mass culture that surrounds him on every side.

What is the picture of maturity projected by the technopolis? William Stringfellow calls attention to a different side of the contemporary scene. Not freedom, he says, but unconscious subservience to the principalities and powers of feudalism constitute the life of metropolis. The movement of history is not toward freedom but rather from industrialization to urbanization and then death, because the city is in a state of perishing. "I suggest that the promises of the industrial revolution have not been vindicated in the city and that they are exposed in the city as illusory."[32] Cox, too, is aware of this dimension of urban life, and he insists that the answer is the further desacralization of the world.

Is it really true, then, to say that the motto of the technopolis is "Nothing sacred"? Granted that uncritical religious imputations acting like the superstitious taboos of primitive cultures must be repudiated in order that men can reap the benefits of their skills and knowledge, what serves as the pattern by which man reshapes his world in view of tomorrow? The only answer seems to be man himself. "Man now is what Christ, according to the New Testament, was to the world. He is the new redeemer, the meaning-giving center of this post-Christian era." But as Gabriel Vahanian, who wrote these words, says, "Just as it was difficult ever to be sure of precisely what the will of God entailed, so it is equally difficult to determine which image of man is going to govern man's responsibility for this world."[33] Man himself is the "last idol"—or rather, the images of man forming the basis of decisions are the last idols. And how shall they fall?

In an earlier day one could hold that in the free interchange of ideas, where each man could raise questions, voice objections, and plead for his views, truth was able to manifest and vindicate itself. The recognition that the very machinery meant to protect men against sinister teaching was actually promoting error and concealing truth prompted the conviction that truth could not ultimately be served by trying to "stack the cards" in its favor. This is the basis of the struggle for free speech, a free press, and freedom of assembly. When ideas confronted each other openly, "truth would out."

But whatever hidden presupposition there is in this

theory that truth verifies itself in debate, the picture is clouded by the phenomena of contemporary mass media. Although formal censorship by either state or church is absent, the very means for gathering, "releasing," and presenting the news as well as for expressing editorial opinion prevent many points of view from even getting a hearing. In many communities a monopolistic relation between the single newspaper and the radio or television station further restricts the publication of any views which vary significantly from public opinion in such a way as to threaten its assumptions. In some communities whole segments of the population making up as much as half of the society lack any voice in the mass media.[34] Advertising budgets have been known to exert financial pressures on editors and station managers. The publication of books has become so costly that only a high volume sale can make it financially feasible. Hence the disenfranchised, the poor, and those with unusual views find it hard to get a hearing. Furthermore, with the advent of motivation research and its employment in so many facets of life from political campaigns to the sale of detergents, the techniques of persuasion are so complicated that an amateur stands scarcely a chance. Even a congressman cannot always be sure whether he is receiving a genuine sampling of his constituents' views or the results of a highly organized letter writing campaign. While there have always been radical differences in the opportunities that men have had to make themselves heard, the advent of mass communication has brought with it a crisis of unforeseen problems.

But it is not only a matter of getting all views into a genuine marketplace of ideas, for today is the age of the specialist, who on the basis of his superior knowledge and experience—or assumed superiority—can silence hosts of ordinary people whose views can be quickly dismissed as uninformed opinion. Although facts in themselves cannot determine what shall be done with or about them, so that the expert can only tell us how to implement a policy which his experience may not help create, the tendency is to confuse the roles. Thus doctors are called on to decide the question of euthanasia, or social workers the morality of birth control.

All this is to say that the process of desacralization is hardly an assured one. True, certain aspects of daily life have lost their religious aura. The resulting freedom is a benefit to be enjoyed. But other aspects of life assume dimensions of the sacred. The task of overthrowing idols is a continual one and its most dangerous dimensions are perhaps yet to be met. If Christianity began the process of desacralization, it bears responsibility for seeing it through anew in each generation.

CHAPTER IV

The Living Body of Christ

Sanctification, the realization of the new humanity of Christ in each man, is God's work. This means that the Christian life is not simply a program of intelligent reform, but that it has its source and dynamic in God. How does God carry this on? Certainly not without us—not without our decision of faith or our working too. "God is at work in you, both to will and to work for his good pleasure," Paul wrote to the Philippians; therefore, "work out your own salvation." Yet the Christian life is no accident. It is a disciplined ordering of thought and activity directed toward Christian maturity.

DIVINE ACTION AND SACRAMENTAL PRESENCE

To speak about the action of God in this world as some sort of extramundane manifestation is impossible in contemporary categories. Either such divine activity becomes part of the total scheme of nature or else it is psychologized as the product of man's mind. If God's action is to have meaning outside of the whole concourse of nature, it can only be through human activity. To use Luther's words, God reveals himself "in, with, and under" the realities of this world, not by supplanting them. This means that no act can be isolated in an exclusive sense as God's act.

Traditionally, Christians have spoken about God's *sacramental* presence as something distinct from either confronting a Thing among things (or Person among persons) or using "God" as a term for some experience which could just as well be spoken of in other ways. Through the Sacraments the power of God was made available for the Christian life. *God* acted in Baptism to incorporate the candidate into the body of Christ giving him spiritual birth. And *God* acted in the Eucharist to give the recipient the food of immortality by which he would become godlike.

This view of sacramental presence was a Neoplatonic interpretation of the Biblical material concerning Baptism and the Lord's Supper. According to this view, all things are contained within the One from "whence" they derive, and thus they symbolize the One. The most complete presentation of the Neoplatonic view is given in the fifth- or sixth-century writings of Pseudo-Dionysius. By participating in the Sacraments and the "levels" of the church, one participates in that greater reality of which these are symbols. This deeper participation does not depend upon a rational understanding and explanation of the connection between the two realms. The reality is "in" and "with" the symbol. The symbol does not merely point to a reality beyond itself: it participates in it. To go through Baptism is to be incorporated into the mystical body of Christ.[1] Baptism was thus not simply a sign of such incorporation for the theologically astute, much less a seal to one's own belief. Bestowing the Sacraments actually brought the saving action of God to men whether they understood what was happening or not.

Nominalism broke that connection, for implied in it was the divinity of all nature. Neoplatonism has always verged on pantheism in such a way as to compromise the freedom of God. Thus, symbols *must* point to God whether he "chooses" to reveal himself or not. But in denying this immediate connection, nominalism had to substitute a purely rationalistic connection between sign and meaning. In a full-blown nominalism a thing is simply what it is and nothing more. By arbitrary designation it can be a sign of another reality, as when an octagonal red plate is a sign that traffic must stop for a through street. But in and of itself it "points to" no further meaning. One who understands the key to a given system of signs can appreciate the other reality with which they are associated, but the connection is not real, only conventional.

Here was one important root of the theological problem which erupted with the Reformation and which radically divided the Lutheran from the Zwinglian branches of the Reformation itself. The tendency of Zwinglianism was to make the connection between the bread and wine of the Lord's Supper and the body and blood of Jesus Christ rational. That is, these elements in the congregational setting helped Christians recall the upper room and Calvary and the great sacrifice by which Christ welded his followers into a single body. Conceivably, if one's imagination were alert, he could dispense with the material signs, the elements of bread and wine. His link to Christ was through his mind, not through matter participating in ultimate reality.

Genuine, living symbols are never those whose power depends upon their being explained. Most of the reputed symbolism in church buildings today is not genuine symbol at all just because it must be explained. It may be a sign to those who possess the key, but it is enigma to everyone else. Only a fairly technical explanation involving the Greek alphabet and vocabulary, for example, can link the fish (*ichthus*) to Christ. To an increasingly urban civilization, even sheaves of wheat and grape vines require rationalistic explanations.

Genuine symbols speak with immediacy. An example might be the popular print *Praying Hands* by Albrecht Dürer. This work is used in bas-relief to decorate chapel walls, as a print on church bulletins and calendars, as a gold embossing on Christmas cards and personal stationery, and even as plaster figurines. Regardless of Dürer's original intention, the *Praying Hands* expresses man's own religiousness and is thus the symbol par excellence of the age of Schleiermacher and his followers. This symbol does not have to be explained (although there is the explanation of Dürer immortalizing the self-sacrifice of his friend). Its appeal is immediate, suggesting a richness of meaning that cannot be conveyed in propositional language. Although the cross, crucifix, and pelican may no longer speak directly to contemporary men, the *Praying Hands* does.

Although the nominalistic point of view dominates our time—linked as it is to the desacralization of the world—the depths of Neoplatonic symbolism have been revived by Freud and his followers through psychoanalysis. David Bakan, for example, interprets Freud through the tradition of Jewish mysticism.[2] Once more, nothing is simply itself. Every act, thought, and word has a deeper significance inseparably tied to it, not one assigned by convention. Only now the reality is not some transcendent realm of ideas or the logos, much less the all-embracing One, but the psyche itself in all its complexity. Whether on a Freudian basis one can develop a new battery of symbols is problematic, since what is one man's symbol of life may be another man's symbol of death, depending upon his early experience. Carl Jung has tried to explore the realm of common symbols, but his conclusions are widely disputed.

Although what the ultimate base of such symbolism may be—such as the depths of human existence as many today suggest—it is generally acknowledged that meanings can be conveyed and retained other than on a conscious, rational level. In other words, it may not be necessary to affirm a Neoplatonic doctrine of symbols as the sole alternative to a rationalistic key. In fact, a universal symbolism intelligible immediately to all would deny the historical role of Christian faith. What the meaning of specific symbols is, however, depends upon the community in which they are used. Thus the *Praying Hands* could in one context mean man's utter dependence upon God, but in the context of contemporary religiosity can mean man himself being religious.

When Russian churchmen visited the United States several years ago they were asked what freedom they had at home to teach Christian doctrine. They answered—though not to the satisfaction of the Americans who had an entirely different perspective—that the Russian church has not depended upon formal teaching but on the religious atmosphere of the home and on the impact of the liturgy itself. The meanings involved are not on the rational level and are therefore not necessarily dissipated by the familiar sort of atheistic propaganda. Such "teaching" goes on in spite of prohibitions against religious classes. Of course the question must be raised as to whether Christianity can be conveyed wholly through such a medium, but one can also ask whether it can be conveyed apart from that medium.

Feuerbach tried to account for the continuing significance of the Christian Sacraments in a rationalistic age in terms of the basic human necessities of food and water. But is the Christian only affirming the conditions of human existence? Hardly, because he knows that the new man lives by the Word of God. That Word overcomes human hostility and alienation, enabling men to live by the reality of God's forgiveness in the face of their own and the world's sin. The presence of God is not in bread and wine or in a hierarchy but with the congregation of God's people. Here the reality of reconciliation is made manifest and acknowledged; here what is proclaimed in the gospel is accomplished; here the first fruits of the Spirit are born. The Christian is not called to *bring* God into the world by engaging in a program or embracing a cause. He is called to *celebrate* God's presence in the fact of reconciliation.

It is for this reason that Stringfellow castigates those who thought that making people Christian depended upon making them Western (the mistake of earlier mission programs) or who today think that making people Christian means making them middle class (the mistake of too much church activity among the poor). In a review of Bruce Kenrick's *Come Out the Wilderness,* the story of the East Harlem Parish, he said that the basic question was whether the Bible was to be accessible to the people of Harlem. Those who established the parish were not primarily motivated by the power of the gospel, he wrote. They had to learn this through their work. "The story of the East Harlem Parish begins like the story of the mere establishment of a settlement house in the slums. It continues through the struggle to differentiate secular charity from love, settlement houses from churches, ideology from theology, social planning from Christian witness and mission, ecclesiastical politics from recognition of the authority and reliability of the indigenous laity."[3]

"Knowing the presence of the Word of God in the world, being made a new person by the power of that

Word, the Christian's task is to so enjoy the Word in the world as to attest the veracity of the Word of God for all men in any and every event."[4] Worship is the celebration of this reality: in the Eucharist, God reconciles the world with himself. "In reality, the Christian bears the tension between the gospel and the world in radical and transforming witness only because he participates in the event of the congregation. It is that event which enables him to witness while dispersed in the world."[5] The Eucharist is not the result of the purely human establishment of unity nor is it a tool to bring about unity, says Bishop John A. T. Robinson, but it confronts us with the perfect unity of Christ and in that unity men do become one.[6]

THE REDISCOVERY OF THE CHURCH

In times past, the evidence that a gathering of men was indeed the community of reconciliation has been sought in organizational and cultic continuity (the Petrine or apostolic successions), in doctrinal purity (Eastern and Protestant orthodoxy), or in certain spiritual signs (from deeds of agapeic love to speaking in tongues). The trouble with these has not been so much that they were wrong in themselves but that given exclusive emphasis they led to false conclusions. In different dimensions, all insist on the *continuity* of the church from one age to another, a continuity different from that of the human community at large, yet related to it.

The continuity of any community is its history. It becomes something different from what it was when it forsakes or repudiates its definitive history. The Christian community identifies itself with the people of God in the Biblical revelation, specifically with the apostolic community of Christ. Whether in all cases it actually shows itself to be the heir of this history is another question. Why it should seek to connect itself with that history is also another question. But that this is its history is its affirmation (confession) of faith, whether it adequately understands the history and its contemporary implications or not.

The recovery for the church of that history after rationalism had virtually dissipated it in the "religion of reason" is the story of the past century or so. In part it depends upon the work of the historians who sought the connection between the new theologies and their Biblical roots. But it also depends upon the liturgical movement which sought to restore the integrity of work, study, and prayer in the life of the church.[7] To restore the unity of life and worship, the question of what the church is in the world by its divine call must be answered. The Reformation, for example, emphasized the corporate nature of worship as against the actor-spectator atmosphere characterizing the late medieval Mass. This found expression in the use of the vernacular for the liturgy, congregational hymns, and actual communion in the Lord's Supper. The gathering of Christ's people around the table often replaced the "celebration" at a high altar. In the theology of justification, the church does not plead for mercy because its very existence is the evidence of God's mercy. Its very coming together as a community is the fact of reconciliation which God has wrought.

Today the demand is frequently made for the "translation" of the liturgies into contemporary language. Bishop Robinson, in spite of his other radical suggestions, thinks this is wrong, that a liturgy from another age rules out a literalistic interpretation and allows each person freedom in understanding.[8] Some have tried to set the traditional

words to modern music, not always successfully.[9] Others
see the problem not only in modern versus Cranmer's
English, for example, but in the figures of speech and
imaginative pictures used. "All we like sheep have gone
astray" has profound meaning for those who know at first
hand sheep's headstrong stupidity, but it is lost on those
who think only of woolly lambs or charming pastoral
scenes. Still others note that form and content are so in-
tegrally related that modern language and modern theology go together, demanding a wholly new approach to
worship.

The matter of hymns is a case in point. It is no accident
that the popular ones, with few exceptions, come from the
Reformation or the Evangelical Revival. During those periods poetry as a whole was cast in regular meter with set
rhyming patterns. It frequently "told a story" or expressed
in variations a recognizable theme which could be trans-
lated into prose. That is not the case today. For a modern
poet to write a recognizable hymn means deliberately
aping a style from the past. Even if it is undertaken, the
result is not likely to be vibrant and fresh.

The question as to what forms of worship are appropriate to the church in our day is more than a matter of
taste: it is a matter of clarifying what the church is meant
to be in the world. The observation that although Jesus
had preached the Kingdom of God the church emerged
instead had characterized a good deal of the liberal attitude toward the church. The reality of Christian faith lay
in personal relationship with God manifest in society, it
was said. The attempt to redefine the church in terms of
its Biblical history occupied theological attention in the
two decades following the outbreak of World War II.
Works on Biblical theology in new perspective[10] were ac-

companied by others pointing up the implications of this study for the doctrine of the church.[11]

As against the tendency of liberalism to stress evolutionary development at the expense of the continuing significance of the past, such books clarified the connection between Israel and the church. They showed that there can be no Biblical Christology without a corresponding doctrine of the church. There is no Messiah apart from a messianic community, no Son of Man without the "saints of the Most High" whom he represents, no "servant of the Lord" without the people of his redemption. It was through the Biblical understanding of God's call of Israel in relation to his total purpose that the way was prepared for the present-day emphasis on mission as the true nature of the church.

This Biblical history is not claimed by the church as its exclusive possession but is proclaimed as the heritage of all men. As Karl Barth puts it, "The goal in the direction of which the true church proceeds and moves is the revelation of the sanctification of all humanity and human life as it has already taken place *de jure* in Jesus Christ."[12] The church is the "congregation or people which knows this elevation and establishment, this sanctification, not merely *de jure* but already *de facto,* and which is therefore a witness to all others, representing the sanctification which has already come upon them too in Jesus Christ."[13] But this representation is only provisional in that it must point to the reality in Jesus Christ amid its own ambiguity. The church represents the sanctification which is *in Christ,* not in itself.

The intention of Barth here to avoid defining the church as an "in-group" opposed to an "out-group" is clear. In appropriating the doctrine of election from the

Calvinist tradition, Barth insists that it means the election of all men, thus rejecting the doctrine of eternal reprobation except as a sort of absolute negation of sin rather than of certain men. The words Barth has used suggest a reversion to the "essence prior to existence" principle of Platonism which is borrowed by many others who try to distinguish between those within and those outside the church only on the basis that the one group "knows" or "acknowledges" the reality of its life in Christ while the other does not. Thus the task of the community would seem to be to pull away the veil, revealing the perpetual truth of divine election. On the contrary, the move from *de jure* to *de facto* is not just insight, but deed—repentance, conversion, faith.

SACRAMENTAL CHURCH AND CHURCH AS SACRAMENT

Seeing the church as the witness to God's presence in the world can avoid certain problems of mistaken identity. One of these has been to regard the church as lord of the earth. The other has been to regard it as the voluntary association of like-minded men.

The first developed in those years when world culture imposed on the church the framework of two worlds—this one and the next, the natural and the supernatural, the temporal and the eternal. The concern of religion was to effect the transmission of the soul from this world to the next. The church, then, was the agency which brought about that transmission. To do this it had the power of God from the world beyond available in the Sacraments, which it dispensed through a divinely authorized priesthood. This meant that the real, working, or active church was the clergy. The laity were passive recipients of the means of grace and salvation.

It must be kept in mind that the sacramental ministry of the church was regarded as the saving agent. Baptism, for example, was itself effective in the regeneration of a man, altering his outlook while making him a member of the church. In medieval woodcuts the church is frequently pictured as Peter's bark, the ship of salvation. The image is useful in understanding this conception. Men can be saved from drowning by being brought out of the sea aboard a ship, whether they understand its destination and its secrets of navigation or not. When the church understood itself as the ship of salvation it did not scruple to use force if necessary to save men, just as today doctors ally themselves with government power to "save" men from illnesses against which they would not otherwise protect themselves. Augustine quoted the command in the parable, "Compel people to come in" (Luke 14:23), as dominican authorization for the use of secular power in the Christian mission.

Because this view of the two worlds was part of the general cultural scene from which the church absorbed it, it was easily assumed that secular power should concern itself with religion. That is, the state should aid and abet the supernatural function of the church. This is the thinking which gave rise to the "Constantinian Age" in which secular power was allied with the church and which, but for the Anabaptists, dominated even Reformation thought. To bring people into the church by prestige if not sheer force was to serve their interests in the best sense of the word. This meant that the secular structures of the world received their significance from their contribution to the task of the church.

The laity consequently occupied a decidedly inferior role in the church. In the first centuries of the Christian era, the general social and philosophical distinction between enlightened and ordinary men found its way into the church with the distinction between the clergy and the laity as part and parcel of the two-worlds doctrine. But the laity still had an active task: they witnessed to the faith in times of persecution. In fact, the witness of the martyrs at times rivaled the sacramental ministry of the church. To die steadfast in the faith was a second baptism—all sins were wiped out and one was assured direct access to heaven. The intercession of the martyrs was eagerly sought by others, so that the martyr cult threatened the established hierarchy of the church. With the end of persecution and the clericalization of the church, there was little for the layman to do.[14]

Against this dominance of the clergy developed an anticlericalism asserting the significance of the secular orders of society in their own right. To use Paul Tillich's language, an antithetical relationship between secular independence (autonomy) and clerical control (heteronomy) cannot be resolved unless both are superseded in theonomy. "In clericalism the church usurps the place of the world; in secularism the world usurps the place of the church."[15] Theonomy in this sense means that God's relation to the world is not through the church alone, but both church and world are responsible to him, though not in the hierarchical arrangement of "spiritual" over "secular." Not every assertion of secular autonomy is a faithless departure from God (as anticlericalism is so often misinterpreted), for it may only parallel the faithless departure already taken by clericalism. That all things are put under the feet of Christ may be good New Testament teaching, but that all things should be under the control of the clergy is teaching with a different source indeed.

If the church is the witness to God's presence in the

world, then the one-sided emphasis on the gathering of the church (*ekklēsia*) from all races, nations, and peoples must be countered by an emphasis on the church as the servant of God's mission to the world (*diaspora*). The church is not simply the company of the saved, seeking to increase itself, but the proclaimer of Christ's Lordship *in the world*.

The Lordship of Christ in the world is exerted not through the church as a clerically dominated institution, however, but in the world's own structures. The same problem which the early church wrestled with in Christology (God and man in Jesus Christ), and which the Reformation dealt with in terms of justification (God's grace and man's work in the Christian life), is now met in the context of church and society. This wider dimension was implicit even in the Christological form of the problem, because it was not completely certain whether Christology was dealing with a man (Jesus of Nazareth) or with mankind (the new humanity); for the reality of the new humanity manifest in Jesus is the new humanity which all men are to become because they are already this in Christ. Nineteenth-century Christologies, in trying to express this universal dimension, frequently sound like sheer immanentism. Indeed, the proclamation of Christ's Lordship does mean an in-historicization of the Christian hope.

Bonhoeffer consciously deals with this problem in defining the church. Had Jesus been a teacher or prophet, followers would have sufficed. But as the *incarnate* Son of God he must have a body.[16] Whereas traditional thought has regarded the incarnation as taking place eternally in the sense that through the ascension Christ remains the God-man throughout eternity, Bonhoeffer thinks of his possessing a body *on earth*. This body is the church, for although all men are with Christ through the incarnation,

Christians are with him in the special sense of being "in Christ" in the totality of their lives. In this sense the church is a "person,"[17] for the new humanity is one, not many. "Through his Spirit, the crucified and risen Lord exists as the Church, as the new man. It is just as true to say that his Body is the new humanity as to say that he is God incarnate dwelling in eternity."[18] Yet Christ stands over against the church as its head.

A doctrine does not occupy space, but the body does in order to proclaim his Word in daily life as well as in liturgy and order. The reality effected by Baptism is the truth by which the Christian lives; it is the truth which sets itself against the structures of the world per se. In this early work, Bonhoeffer thought that meant the Christian would not revolt against earthly powers since revolution is but one more structure of the world. While the original disciples were called to leave everything to follow Jesus, now that Christ's body has penetrated the world, discipleship means living "in Christ" in the world. Still, this is not to endorse the prevailing powers, because *all* forms of this world are being challenged. Let the Christian remain in the world, wrote Bonhoeffer, "to engage in frontal assault on it, and let him live the life of his secular calling in order to show himself as a stranger in this world all the more."[19] The very life of the Christian community is testimony to the fact that the fashion of this world passes away (I Cor. 7:31).

Yet in his experience with the Nazi regime, Bonhoeffer came to see that living "in Christ" does mean entering into the struggle of secular structures. As against the view of the church as the ark of salvation, then, can be set the view of it as agent in the "politics of God." Although the emphasis is fresh in our time through the ethical teaching of

Paul Lehmann and Harvey Cox, the idea is quite centrally Biblical. The scene of God's activity in the Bible is not simply the church or Israel but the whole world. The purpose of his activity is to "keep human life human," to use Lehmann's phrase. The crucial Biblical images are all political: people, covenant, slavery, land, law, judge, king, etc.[20] In spite of man's inversion of God's order, God ever afresh manifests the new community. The penultimate chapter of Biblical history is the eucharistic community of the church in the world, the laboratory of maturity.[21]

Lehmann cites three examples of how this Biblical perspective was kept alive even during those years when the two-world metaphysic debilitated Christian social witness. Against gnostic schemes of salvation, the doctrine of the Trinity affirmed that the Redeemer is one with the Creator, so that the scene of his work is this world, not some realm beyond. Calvin, in his emphasis on the threefold office of Christ, sought to maintain the connection between the Mediator and the Messiah, between Christ and his people. Christ's prophetic role is to keep his people aware of the signs of his messianic activity; his priesthood has ethical rather than cultic significance; and his Kingship, while not emphasized by Calvin because of contemporary dangers of political anarchy, means that the whole world must be seen in terms of the victory of Christ.[22] While the church is peculiarly his people, in other words, his work extends to all men. And in the doctrines of the Second Adam and Second Advent, the reality of human maturity has been asserted as a present fact from which all life is to be understood: it is not merely a future event or ideal.[23]

Ever since Augustine understood the church through the parable of the net gathering fish of every kind from the sea for a separation ashore of the good and bad (Matt. 13:47–

50), the hope to make the earthly church a haven of purely ideal existence has had to defend itself against charges of theological unreality and Christian irresponsibility. Instead, there has been a recognition that the proper place for the church is in the world, working with and through imperfect men. The orientation to mission per se, then, is not new. But what is new is a recognition of the need for different tactics as a result of the desacralization of the world. The difference is that instead of the state and other institutions of the world being subservient to the church, making the church's work easier by bringing or forcing men into it, they are now held to be independent and the task of the church is to serve the world in and through the world's own forms. Its purpose is not to supplant the structures of the world but to enable them to fulfill their own functions. In other words, the Christian's question is not, How can I use this secular job to aid the church? but, How can I fulfill Christ's purpose for it?

It should be obvious that throughout the discussion, the meaning of "church" has not remained constant. We can say that it was a particular understanding of the "church" that identified it with the hierarchical institution. Today the problem is more complicated, for although Protestantism has repudiated the hierarchical definition of the church, there is still an organizational, institutional reality to deal with over and above God's people as they are active in the world. Christians can be ever so busy in daily life, in the struggle over social issues, and in their personal relationships, but unless the ecclesiastical organizations involve themselves in some conspicuous activity, the "church" is said to be doing nothing.

This ambiguity of the word may indicate a failure of the "church" to find forms suitable to its contemporary mission. Many who are concerned for church renewal have not faced the full implications of this possibility. Thus, Robert A. Raines with italics: *"The first thing to reaffirm is that we must stick with the church."*[24] But is "the church" the present denominational congregations? The hierarchical form of the church was appropriate when the church was understood as transmitting heavenly grace to men. But when this view was rejected at the Reformation, changes in organizational form resulted, e.g., the attempt to express the priesthood of all believers through the Presbyterian pattern of lay eldership. Today the organizational lines of the church again run counter to much understanding of its mission. Colin Williams has called attention to the fact that present-day church structures are primarily based on the residential parish. But whereas these once meant the communities where men lived, worked, and played, now they are frequently little more than bedroom suburbs. Because of economic and racial structuring of residence communities, a church so oriented necessarily reinforces the social stratification of today's world. New forms must be devised along quite different lines.[25]

Such a "church" might be fluid in its structure as groups form for a limited time and then regroup in terms of a different interest or purpose. If the parish is retained—and it is hard to see how Christian education of children and youth, to cite one example, could go on without it—it must rethink its whole internal organization in view of the necessity of training laymen for their Christian mission in the world.

The danger in this view is that the church may become only a series of interest groups, each united within itself by its special interest and thereby separated from all others. If life "in Christ" is real, it must bridge gaps between people who are concerned as Christians with race relations, others working for world peace, others who focus attention on Christianity and the arts, some who worship with the music of Bach, and others who worship with folk song or jazz. At one time when the parish comprised the rich and poor, landholders and merchants, tradesmen and nobles in a given locality, it expressed, however imperfectly, the power of Christ to break down human barriers in the eucharistic reality of reconciliation. Today when "churches" are frequently gathered on the basis of human preferences and therefore manifest only fragmentarily the presence of God, the reality of unity awaits adequate expression.

THE CHURCH AS LAITY

When the reality of the church is no longer understood to center in the clergy and its supernatural function, then the role of each member becomes crucial. The laity is no longer merely the passive recipient of supernatural benefits but constitutes the active life of the church. Hans-Ruedi Weber in the influential book *The Militant Ministry*[26] calls attention to the military terminology used by the early church. Instead of emphasizing the ministry of the clerical hierarchy to the church, it points to the ministry of the whole church to the world. Baptism is the military oath, station is a battle position, pagans are civilians. Thus, Baptism is the ordination of *all* Christians to their task. The function of this "army," according to Weber, is to represent Christ as the victorious king in the whole inhabited world—occupying the land he has conquered, heralding his victory, and establishing the marks of peace and reconciliation. Just as the emperor had to equip his army and maintain its morale, so Christ provides for the equipment of the ministry of the total church. But this army is not oriented toward offense. Its armor is defensive. Its task is to stand fast in territory already won.

The function of the clergy is not to constitute the church but to help the church fulfill its role: "The ministers are given in order that the militant church may really receive and accept its charismatic equipment and put on the armor of God, to see that it does not 'fall out of the domain of grace,' but grow in grace, show forth its particular way of life and fulfill its ministry of gracious service."[27] This ministry is fulfilled through sacrifice patterned on Christ's offering of himself. The church is itself the "victorious victim" which suffers in joy. "The agony of the world is not an illness leading to death, and its longings, revolutions and innovations are not in vain."[28]

Weber's book is striking in its appropriation of the military terminology of the early church. But in 1958, Hendrik Kraemer called attention to the need for a "theology of the laity"—not a manual of Christian beliefs set in lay language, but a theology of the lay role in the church. A new understanding of the laity, he said, is integral to a new understanding of the church which must be defined in terms of mission, not society, of ministry, not The Ministry. It must cease being introverted.

Only when the dimension of the world enters fully into the purview of a doctrine of the Church, when the perennial call for renewal is fully accounted for in it and when the directives for the Church's life and expression are taken from the Church's being and calling, fully aware of the risk this implies, is a genuine theology of the laity (as an indispensable part of the whole doctrine of the Church) possible.[29]

This is not mere humanism, he insists, for the directive of the church is not derived from an analysis of the contemporary scene but from Christ.

The persistence of the practical influence of the hier-

archical concept of the church repudiated by the Reformation can be seen in the fact that not until the Oxford
Conference of 1937 on "Church, Community, and State"
were laymen extensively consulted, although they were influential in the ecumenical movement from its beginning.
In 1948 the laity was one of the subjects of preparatory
study for the organizing meeting of the World Council of
Churches at Amsterdam. In the Department of the Laity's
report to the New Delhi Assembly in 1961 all meanings of
"laity" in terms of a distinction of ranks, jobs, or education in the church were rejected for the straightforward
meaning of the "whole people of God."[30] A theology of the
laity, therefore, "should define and describe in understandable theological terms . . . what it means to see the Church
in this aspect, and therefore what God is calling his people
to be and do."[31] This must be set against theologies of
special privilege, for what God offers is "a share in the sufferings of Christ in and for the world."[32]

This understanding of the church delivers the clergyman
from the attempt to be an expert on nearly everything.
Sermons have frequently been preached on "What the
Christian must do about ————." But if Christian faith is
not to be reduced to the mere inner life and the minister
to a psychological adviser, many areas must be discussed
by Christians in which the clergyman himself is only a
novice. "What the Christian must do" is not given by some
heavenly voice to the clergyman, and so relayed to the
congregation, but it must be learned through the joint
study of laymen themselves.

In replying to suggestions of nonreligious Christianity,
Daniel Jenkins notes that God's Spirit is not "possessed"
by the ecclesiastical institution and that therefore "the believer must try to discover the will of God both in the life

of the Church and in the various spheres of his secular calling."[33] In other words, God is not first given to the church and from there brought to the world, so that men learn God's will in the church and then apply it to the world; rather, the Christian is one who is aware of God's working in both church and world. Both historically and theologically, Christendom is no longer "an executive organ for carrying out the legislation of the church in the world" and in its service in the world it can no longer appeal to the "supernatural authority of the Church."[34] Discerning the will of God in a concrete situation, then, means a joint effort of Christians involved in the situation along with such Biblical scholarship as will help open its meaning.

The task now confronting the church is to train laymen for their work in the world. "To live in this modern world of ours as a Christian cannot be done just by instinct," writes Kathleen Bliss.

It is not something which the Christian immediately discovers by joining in the usual life of the parish. It has to be learned, and such learning is a combination of a deeper understanding of the Gospel and a thorough use of the scientific tools for the study of man and society.[35]

The object of such attempted outreach is not to make individual converts and bring them into the Church (though that may very well be, under God, one of the things that happens) but to put the Church once more into a relationship with society which will enable it to perform its duty towards society as such.[36]

To effect this training, many of the European churches, and increasingly those in America, have instituted lay academies. In the lay academy, Christians whose lives are set in the secular world meet for study and discussion of their own problems in relation to the gospel. Eberhard

Müller in discussing this work in Germany says that the purpose is not to convert but to facilitate the exchange of views between Christians and non-Christians. One of the reasons for such a program is that nonchurchmen are wary of any organization with a "religious" stamp; hence they must be prepared at their own spiritual level for participation in formal extensions of the church in the world.[37] In commenting on the work of Scotland's Iona Community, Ralph Morton writes, "It rests on the conviction that we have to start with the relationship of persons to each other in the immediate situation in which they are set; that it must be in terms of the immediate concern of their lives; and that it must discover immediate patterns of action now."[38] All training of the laity requires a communal life of work, study, and worship, according to Morton. In weekend conferences, Chicago's Ecumenical Institute seeks to interpret the change in theological climate reflected in the works of such men as Bonhoeffer, Bultmann, and Tillich, and help both pastors and laymen see the implications of the new understanding of the function of the church in the world.

But what is it that the layman works for in the world? How does he represent Christ there? There is no question that many see the Christian as the ideal man as the world itself would define him—more civic-minded, more willing to serve various organizations, more philanthropic, and more observant of religious duties. J. Edward Carothers in a book on poverty for study by church groups says: "It may come as a surprise to many that this plea for renewal has not centered around more Bible reading and private prayer nor has it put the emphasis on congregational worship. . . . The call for renewal is generally in the framework of a demand that the churches get into the business of converting society."[39]

In one sense this is true: it is no longer taken for granted that the church can conduct Bible study as a self-contained activity and leave it to the individual Christian to apply it as best he can. But it would be false to say that the movement for renewal does not concern itself with Bible study and prayer but with converting the world instead. To what is the world to be converted? To its own best wisdom? Then what is the dynamic of the movement? What is to spark the realization of its potentiality? The point is rather that Bible study and prayer, divorced from the concerns of the world, are spurious. Christians can approach the Bible authentically only as they bring with them their real life. Only as they consider what God wants them to do here and now are they likely to hear any Word of God.

If what Cox and others have said is right, that it is the Christian gospel which desacralizes the world, then this is the important dimension of "converting the world." If idolatry does not die but resurrects itself in each generation, establishing its hampering taboos of the pseudo sacred, then it is the specific task of Christians to expose and attack these idolatrous forces wherever they appear. But the valid basis of that attack cannot be some value elevated by ignorance or cunning to a supreme position. That can lead only to an inter-idol struggle. For Christians, the only valid basis of attack is the knowledge of the true God revealed in Jesus Christ.

The exposition of what this means takes us back to Weber's *The Militant Ministry*. Its first aspect is the proclamation of Christ's Lordship over the principalities and powers that control human life. In New Testament times these were probably conceived as spiritual "beings." In our era of depopulated heavens, ideologies, institutions, and public images probably convey the meaning better. They exert pressure on men. Each person is aware of the power of what others expect him to be over his action and his own self-expectation. Economic pressures, national or racial images, personality myths—all these bend men to their control. To deny their reality is foolish. But the Christian, knowing Christ's triumph, is free to attack their false claim of absolute authority. Economic factors, though powerful, are amenable to human control for those who do not worship them. The epistle to the Ephesians speaks of the nations apart from Christ "having no hope and without God in the world" (Eph. 2:12). The human ideal, unless it is to be the Promethean taunt of fate, must have a solid foundation if it is not itself to become merely a tool of the principalities and powers.

Weber speaks also of the task of the Christian soldier as establishing the marks of peace and reconciliation. Just as the aim of conquest is to settle down in new order, so the Christian wants to bring about reconciliation. In the New Testament, Christ is proclaimed as having overcome the divisions of men—Jew-Gentile, bond-free, male-female, Greek-barbarian. The Samaritan of the familiar parable fulfills a ministry of reconciliation in tending the wounded man: he acts within the reality of reconciliation, giving it concrete expression. Much is said today about the civil rights struggle in the sense of securing for all men their constitutional—indeed, human—rights. But apart from the structures of law which dare not be minimized, the actual working out of relationships between races and economic groups depends on more than legal rights. While the Christian as citizen demands right secured by law, he is also concerned for that genuine reconciliation which the law is powerless to bring about; but he is not deluded about the foundations in social structure on which reconciliation must be concretely formed.

Ecumenism

For the last several centuries improved communications have made it both possible and necessary for people of different traditions to function together. Regional peculiarities which once appeared to divide men irreconcilably now are seen as only relative, interesting bits of "local color." In this sense, the willingness of national and denominational churches to enter into formal relationships with each other simply manifests the same force toward unification.

Moreover, through mission efforts in undeveloped lands where the doctrinal disputes of the sixteenth and seventeenth centuries mean nothing and in the ministry to the universities where the real confrontation is between the gospel and the world rather than between confessional positions, the necessity of bridging the divisions of the organized church have been increasingly evident. In contrast to the attempt at unification through doctrinal discussion as at the famous colloquy between Luther and Zwingli, modern discussions have been primarily functional in their approach. The modern ecumenical movement began with attempts to coordinate missionary activities and student work. The concern for mission in the broad sense of the word has brought churches together as confessional discussions have tended to separate them.

This concern for mission has led the Roman Catholic Church, in the Second Vatican Council, to modify its intransigent position that Protestants are somehow enemies rather than joint workers with Christ: "The Church recognizes that in many ways she is linked with those who, being baptized, are honored with the name of Christian, though they do not profess the faith in its entirety or do not preserve unity of communion with the successor of Peter. . . . We can say that in some real way they are joined with us in the Holy Spirit, for to them also He gives His gifts and graces."[40] In the Decree on the Apostolate of the Laity, the increasing importance of the laity to the mission of the church is noted. Practically speaking, in many parts of the world the hierarchy cannot function and the church must be maintained solely through lay witness. In this particular decree, all mission of the church is identified with the apostolate which *is* the Christian vocation into which one is incorporated through Baptism.[41] Christ's message is manifested by words of witness and instruction and by deeds in the struggle to apply Christian principles to current problems.

It is this kind of statement about the function of the laity whether from Roman, Orthodox, or Protestant sources that may indicate a shift of emphasis in the ecumenical movement. Whereas to date ecumenism has meant largely a cooperation of *churches,* increasingly it may mean the cooperation of *Christians* in specific local ventures. In commenting on what he calls the "Crisis in the Ecumenical Movement," Albert van den Heuvel writes that just as ecumenical leaders are beginning to work together, the whole movement is bogging down because of the gap between these leaders oriented toward a "church period" and their constituencies which are oriented toward a "personal period." He sees a new group of ecumenists emerging: "I would call this group the secular ecumenists, by which is simply meant that their main ecumenical interest lies in the relation between church and world. They regard the ecumenical movement as pertaining to the relation between church and society rather than the relation of churches among themselves."[42] They see church unity not as a first goal but as a by-product of mission. Genuine unity in this view is functional: "It should allow all those who want to follow the Messiah in his reconciling, crisis-provoking, idol-smashing and humanity-restoring ministry to do so together." Even confessional unity within denominations is a myth today, says van den Heuvel; at best there is only a similar historical orientation.

For example, in a specific community, plans to use the machinery of the urban renewal program may make no provision for the inhabitants of the area to be razed. Christian laymen will be concerned to do something about the situation. They will be motivated by their faith, but their working together will depend on purely functional rather than denominational relationships. Board members of settlement houses, social workers, lawyers, city council members, concerned citizens—all will find themselves brought together by their common concern. Perhaps denominational cooperation can make critical funds available, or legal council, or widespread publicity. It is in this sort of functional unity that many see the true unity of the church. "But active concern with the world—with the sufferings of the poor and needy; with peace; with problems created by rapid social change; with race tensions and the possibility of overcoming them—these are all present as part of the discussion of what it means to be the one people of God in the world,"[43] writes Kathleen Bliss.

This same experience of *functional* unity has also been in the worship of the church. Of course the ecclesiastical strictures against intercommunion still prevail, as well as the firm intention to maintain separate, and to a large extent separating, traditions; but the liturgical movement has frequently brought a new perspective in understanding these separate traditions. A few years ago the "Demonstration English Mass" in the musical setting by Dennis Fitzpatrick, although meant primarily for the education of the

hierarchy and laity of the Roman Catholic Church in relation to the Second Vatican Council, was the occasion of
widely ecumenical participation. Clearly designated as
"demonstration" and without an ordained celebrant, these
could not be regarded as Masses proper. But the singing of
the liturgy, the distribution of the elements, and the "kiss
of peace"—though unofficial—brought people of diverse
traditions together in such a way that many wondered what
more officiality would have added to the occasion apart
from ecclesiastical embarrassment.

The increasing irritation with denominational structures can be seen in laymen who look less and less to them
for inspiration and support, in students who more and
more ignore them, and in ministerial candidates who seek
service outside the traditional parish. To some this means
the waning influence of Christian faith. To others it is the
sign of emerging life of the church. After enumerating
specific areas of possible cooperation among churches, Walter S. Kilpatrick writes:

The ecumenical movement can never be frozen into a world
council of churches, even one with today's intoxicating vision
of pope and patriarch and church president each finding his
place there. . . . If it is to be anything more than a chapter
in church history, it must eventually find its way into the heart
and mind and soul of each Christian in every church. We
must be members one of another.[44]

CHAPTER V

Personal Life in the Body

"When there *is* no church to *go* to, one *can* only *be* the Church."[1] Thus Bishop Robinson emphasizes that the church is not to be defined as a collective but as a life that pulses in each cell of the body. The church is a congregation or parish, it is the few gathered together in a home, it is also the single Christian wherever he goes. Just for this reason the distinction between life as a member of the church and life as an individual Christian is impossible. One's prayers as an individual Christian are nevertheless prayers of the church: to pray as a Christian is to pray with God's people.[2] A Christian life possesses a rhythm of the personal and the communal, and each penetrates the other.

DEVOTION TO CHRIST

As against programs of self-fulfillment, conformity to an ideal, or restructuring by group loyalties, the Christian life has been understood as a personal response to the call of Jesus Christ to follow him in a life lived in fellowship with him. Several years ago newspapers carried a story about certain Negro leaders of the civil rights movement who were despairing about churches' indifference to their cause. Some were quoted as saying that unless the church got solidly behind the movement, Negroes would shift their loyalty from Christianity to Islam. One can understand their frustration with the established churches. But one is Christian not through commitment to a program but rather to Christ. The pattern of that commitment is the permanent relationship of marriage in that all other possibilities of loyalty are surrendered for life. Can there be Christian commitment which does not engage the person of Christ? But how is such personal commitment possible over the gap of two thousand years of history?

Through the past century and a half, the problem of formulating an accurate picture of Jesus has occupied Biblical scholars, theologians, and historians. At one point it seemed as if the efforts of positivistic historians, extracting the genuine historical material of the New Testament from faith statements cast in a quasi-historical form, might succeed. But as Albert Schweitzer so aptly put it, just as we were about ready to embrace the Jesus who had thus come to us over the centuries, he walked right past us back into the first century. In other words, even if the program had succeeded, the real human Jesus of the first century would be more alien to us than we had expected. The historical Jesus is at best an intellectual creation and can no more *meet* us than can the historical Julius Caesar.

Tension between the logos or Christ of faith and the person of Jesus has continued throughout Christian history. Jesus called the disciples to follow him, and if the New Testament records are correct, it was only through their following that they came to understand who he was — that is, came to understand his meaning. They expressed that meaning in the messianic categories of Jewish eschatological hope. But the early and medieval church, in the attempt to define his *universal* significance, spoke

of him as the eternal in time, the logos in history. Christian devotion up to at least the eleventh and twelfth centuries focused not on the historical realities of Jesus' life,
but on the abstraction of becoming godlike—timeless like
his eternity, anchored in the realm beyond time rather than
in this imperfect and perishing world. Devotion sometimes took bizarre forms—Simeon Stylites' pillar existence
or the anchorites' isolation. Meditation on the transitori-
ness of time was an important part of the regimen along
with just those austerities which denied the claim of the
flesh, man's form in time. Jerome in the wilderness was
the subject of many a painting, the saint with his back to
the world, looking into a cave, intent on a skull.

It was the Crusades which brought the concreteness of
Jesus' historical life fresh to the mind of the West. The
change can be seen in Bernard of Clairvaux and the circle
that he influenced. The object of his mysticism is not to
escape time through the logos, the eternal in time; not to
be merged with the barren godhead; but by humility,
deeds of love, and contemplation of the passion of Christ
to be one with *him*. The prototype of god-union in this
world is the historical incarnation itself, the man of sorrows and of love. To be merged with God is not to be
abstracted from time but to join Christ in the passion in
time. Certainly Bernard, who was counselor for bishops
and kings, mediator in the numerous quarrels of feudal
administration, and reformer of the monastic system, could
not be accused of quietism. But others did let the practical
demands of life drown in the copious tears they shed con-
templating the passion. Francis of Assisi rescued the whole
effort from practical irrelevance in his discovery that in
order to know the love of Christ, which was the goal of the
Christian life, he had also to know the pain. The stigmata

were the sacrament of that identification. His lighthearted-
ness and lack of calculation have refreshed Christians ever
since.

The imitation of Christ could be taken quite literally—
going about barefooted, one robe, no purse, no fore-
thought for food or shelter, possessing nothing yet possessing all things—and that was the way the Middle Ages
came to terms with the Jesus of history. Or it might find its
outlet in long vigils in prayer, either in the disciplined
community of a monastery or in the lonely life of the soli-
tary mystic. In a world that was already "Christian" in
both church and government, it was only such activity that
could consume the energies of burning devotion. Where
the issue was drawn—such as the Holy Land in the hands
of infidels, or the sick to tend, the lepers to care for, the
heathen to convert—there the energy could concentrate
itself in practical service. At times it could break loose in
reforming zeal and in its drive for purity could push out
into heresy—as it did with the Cathari and in a less het-
erodox form with the Waldenses.

The Reformation changed some of this but not all. Erasmus and his friends could plead eloquently for the "philosophy of Christ." But personal devotion to Christ was
still the mainspring of Christian life. "What is your only
comfort in life or in death?" asks the very first question of
the Heidelberg (Reformed) Catechism; and the answer:
"That I in body and soul, both in life and in death, am not
my own but belong to my faithful Savior Jesus Christ. . . ."
The dare-all-and-die attitude of romantic medievalism was
challenged to engage specific conflicts with recalcitrant
churches and governments. Following Christ lost some of
the more picturesque elements of Francis and his *joculares,*
but it picked up the rigor of translation into the "vernacu-

lar" of the sixteenth- and seventeenth-century life. Here too there could be repudiation of the world which passes away, but the men of the post-Reformation period recognized that "this world" takes more subtle forms than an extra pair of sandals or arrangements for daily meals. Even Loyola's spiritual exercises were oriented to the new age into which Europe was entering.

The God-initiated endeavor for his lost image traced in human life was the consuming passion of the devotion to Christ in those years. The struggles of faith against distrust and unbelief were worked out, not in bitter loneliness, but in the presence of the Almighty through prayer. And outside the inner life of Sonship there was a world to capture and transform. The Christian was the *miles* of Christ, the soldier of the King whose crown rights were to be proclaimed and honored in the world. This was the new significance of commitment to the historical Jesus. The chasm between the centuries was recognized; hence historical fidelity meant an imaginative engagement of discipleship with an understanding of the unique possibilities of the times. Christ's Kingship meant not the return to conditions of the first century, but a faithfulness in the present oriented toward the future. This meant a church whose very structure acknowledged the priesthood of all believers and provided for confrontation with the living word of God. And it meant a government among Christians in which all bore responsibility in maturity and which not only curbed lawlessness but provided the positive context in which the sons of God could be revealed.

The secularization of that program is the story of our era. The possibilities that had been the marks of the new humanity in Christ were now taken to be possibilities of man in his own right. The specific tie to Jesus of Nazareth began again to dissolve into the ideal of human self-fulfill-ment. Whereas early Christianity fixed its hope on eternity to let time take care of itself, medieval imitation of Christ sought the discipleship of first-century Palestine, and the post-Reformation period tried to follow a living Christ into the new challenges of its own age, the modern period has tended to find its dynamic in the movement of history itself. Jesus of Nazareth in his historical concreteness is only the example of a type: what is sought is the "Christ" beyond who is incarnate in each age and therefore uniquely relevant to it. Discipleship is obedience "as he was obe-dient."[3]

Yet this is no simple story of progressive infidelity. For if the medieval Jesus could speak compassion from such agony as characterizes the Isenheim altarpiece, and if the Reformation Christ could win and command men's loyal-ties from the living Word in the Bible, the Christ of today speaks from within the personal relationship of those who find themselves bound together in their common concerns. Bonhoeffer speaks of the "man for others." William Hamil-ton agrees: "Jesus is Lord by being servant; to be Lord and to be servant are the same."[4] John J. Vincent says that young people today cannot understand his Saviorhood but can respond to his call to serve.[5] Discipleship, not encoun-ter, is the emphasis. And yet where personal loyalty is en-gaged, the personal Christ cannot be absent.

There are dangers in such a reinterpretation, of course. But there have been dangers in every attempt to wrestle seriously with Christian discipleship. The Neoplatonic Christ of Nicaea and Chalcedon could give every moment of time significance as symbol of eternity: he also could negate the significance of time as the very opposite of eter-nity. The suffering Christ of the Middle Ages could call men to a faith working by love that humanized the remains of Roman society and tamed the barbarians, but he could also call men to preoccupation with inwardness that irresponsibly lost touch with the world of men. The Reformation Christ of the Word could call men to new obedience fitted to the time, but he could also let loose the passions of fanaticism that decimated Europe. The "man for others" can lead us to responsible maturity or he can allow us to fritter away our heritage of church and Bible.

THE LIVING WORD

The balance and perspective required to disengage such aberrations of an age's image of Christ are not given by that age itself. Kenneth Hamilton in discussing the relation between Altizer and Cox to the twin themes of old liberalism writes: "The root of the matter is that we hold fast to Christ, and not to any Christ who may happen to appeal to the contemporary religious consciousness, but to the Word made flesh, the Son of the Living God."[6] What frees the Christian from total slavery to the moment is not that he is also a citizen of eternity and can thus bring an absolute judgment to each moment of time, however, but that he has a history which binds him to all ages. That history is given him in the tradition of the church for which the Bible is the canon—the standard, rule, or measure.

Calvin says in the *Institutes* that nature does not suffice to teach us of God and his will and that God has taught us himself by opening "his own holy mouth" in Scripture.[7] Yet the truth of Scripture is "sealed to our hearts" only by the inner witness of the Holy Spirit, not simply commended to us by an ecclesiastical institution.[8] But there has always been a problem of correlating Christianity as a religion of the book and as a religion of the Spirit. Both Protestantism and Catholicism have emphasized the au-

thority of the Bible. The Bible thus constitutes the definitive tradition so that to show that something is Biblical is
to show that it belongs to the mainstream of Christian
faith and life.

But the connection of the present moment with the
Scriptural word is not simple precisely because there is no
Scriptural word as an entity in and of itself apart from
interpretation. In facing the double question "What does
the Bible say?" and "Is it true?" Christians are prone to
answer the first in terms of the second. What Scripture
really says, as against prevailing views and practices of a
given period, is always itself influenced by the age which is
trying to learn its meaning. The Scriptural word that was
cited by the Reformers was not some static possession of
the church which once again was brought out, read, and
implemented, like the scroll discovered in Josiah's reha-
bilitation of the Temple. It was Scripture as it spoke to the
issues of the sixteenth century. The basis of their interpretation of what Scripture "really says" was not some
perspective *sub specie aeternitatis* but the tradition of the
church (though not necessarily of the curia) in which they
stood. It was this concrete situation in the continuing
history of the church rather than any formal principles of
hermeneutics which made Scripture come to life, authentically speaking God's word of judgment and reconciliation.

The same must be said today, particularly as it concerns
the layman. For the last century so much has been said
and written about the historical and critical problems of
Scripture that one might think it had been given to a
special group of scholars. While it is of course true that
historical and critical problems requiring special study are
involved in any sound interpretation of a text, the crucial
historical perspective is that furnished by the whole tradition in which the Christian stands. The important devel-

opments of lay Bible study in the past two decades such as those undertaken in writings by Suzanne de Dietrich[9] have been effective not so much because they delivered technical information to the ordinary Christian but in that they brought the layman within the circle of historical continuity. They helped him see that the Biblical story is also his story, or his story because it is God's story. One has only to contrast the vividness of today's approach to those of a generation ago, concentrating as they did on literary analysis or evolutionary perspective, to see the difference.

Such an approach to the Bible puts a severe strain on the educative processes of the church in order that what the Christian brings to his Bible-reading is the authentic tradition and not some spurious cultural voice of the moment that knows nothing of belonging to a people of God extending through the ages. Of course he will "interpret" the Scripture he reads. At times he will need help to recapture the cultural situation in which it was written or to which it first spoke. Its living concreteness *then* is necessary to its concreteness *today*. Were it abstract then, it would also be abstract today. And he must be helped to appreciate the various circumstances in the history of the church to which it has ever spoken afresh. But all this will form the general background out of which Scripture speaks the living word of God, now in devotional reading, now in a Bible-study class, now in the perplexities of personal decision, now in the specific task of preaching, now in the face of death itself.

Because in worship the community reaffirms its identity in the continuity of God's people between the past and the future, the Scriptural word in worship is important. Scripture is given to that community. There it is clear that its function is not to settle questions of scientific interest, not to provide information for a compilation of ancient history, not to illustrate the evolution of religious concepts, but to guide and interpret the life of that community. But wherever Christians by their acts and words seek God's guidance through his living relationship with his people, there is the church involved in preaching and hearing God's word. The Scripture records the definitive part of the history of contemporary Christians. Apart from it, they become something different. This does not mean that by turning to the pages of the Bible the "Biblical answer" for various questions can be learned. It means that an answer is related not only to a problem but to a people in a situation facing a problem. What they work out in that concrete situation depends upon who they know themselves to be in addition to their knowledge of the situation.

Devotional reading of Scripture does not take place apart from this context of community identity. Although one person ought not to look to that community to provide his own identity or the solutions to all his problems, nothing that he does can be in utter isolation from that community. In devotional reading he joins that community. Whatever value there may be in such techniques of devotional reading is derived from that wider context. It is a "recalling to mind." If it is not to become a fetish ("a verse a day keeps trouble away"), it must be within the context of the Christian community which it in turn supports.

CHRISTIAN NURTURE

Obviously the Christian heritage is mediated through the life of the church itself—the services of worship, church school, membership classes, celebration of the Sacraments, observations of the church year, service projects, and family devotional life. But there are also dimensions mediated through Western culture itself. Abraham Lincoln had little formal religious training, but by the very attitudes of the community at large, he was encouraged to read the Bible and ponder its meanings. There was a time when the Bible would be on any list of the "If I had to choose only five books" sort, whether the person drawing it up regarded himself as a believer or not.

Today, except for wistful glances at the past, this is no longer likely to be true. And the loss is significant not only to the church but to the culture which loses its grasp of the goals by which it orders its activity. In the mounting suspicion of any sort of sectarian instruction in the public schools, the Bible has ceased to be read there to any significant extent. Pageants and plays at Christmastime and on other festival occasions are losing specific Christian character to become "community celebrations" acknowledging the religious pluralism of American society. Where churches have not simply capitulated to the "Protestant-Catholic-Jew" amalgam of American religiosity they have tried to extend religious instruction through weekday sessions. In some communities cooperative ventures using "released time" from the school day have been successful. Where the church has sought not merely to add a course in religious instruction but to present the whole curriculum from a religious point of view, the possibilities of "shared time" have been explored. In this program, students attend the public school for those classes and activities requiring expensive equipment and the parochial school for other subjects.

But others, fearing the social divisiveness of such practices see hope only in a general, objective program of religious instruction integrated with the curriculum. On the basis of the distinction between talking about religion and forcing students to participate in religious observances, they hold that the way is clear to bring religion legitimately into the school curriculum which must concern itself with the whole of life.[10] The wider dimensions of this problem are only beginning to be seen, however, for public school instruction is but one aspect of it. In higher education the part played by church colleges is rapidly decreasing in comparison with the state and private secular universities and their curricula are becoming more alike. Dr. Leonard Swidler, of Temple University, argues that the answer in this situation is elective ecumenical theological instruction on the undergraduate level. Here the dangers of indoctrination, acute with children, are far less serious because an objective stance can be taken.[11] Justice Clark in regard to the Supreme Court decision regarding religious exercises in the public schools has said that the comparative study of religion or study of the Bible for its historical and literary qualities is certainly in place in a total educational program. Dean Price, of the Harvard Graduate School of Public Administration, has pointed out that with science alone we lack a sense of purpose for existence and thus have nothing to determine our political goals.[12] Whether the Christian heritage can be conveyed through objective teaching about it without that position itself implying a religious commitment opposing specifically Christian commitment is problematic. The attempt is a modern form of Socinianism which assumes that by an impartial survey of the materials open to reason one can find all the truth he needs.

As yet Christians have not learned to use mass media particularly effectively, especially when their use of movies, radio, and television is compared to their use of printing in the sixteenth and seventeenth centuries. "Religious" motion pictures have often been an embarrassment to Christian leaders, and pietistic moralism has prevented a full use of genuinely artistic productions which challenge thought and faith. Newsweeklies have brought the "death of God" discussion to popular attention, and its leading spokesmen have appeared in television interviews. A televised Bible course has been popular. Several situational presentation series have been produced to stimulate thought and conversation. One has been specifically directed to children. Occasional documentary programs have dealt with social problem areas and have depicted various agencies of the church at work. In recent years, newspaper "religion" pages are less likely to have Sunday school lesson outlines on them than reports of genuine news and developments on the wider scene of the meeting between church and society.

Near the end of *The Old Faith and the New* written toward the close of his career, David F. Strauss suggested that the Scriptures were not necessary inspiration for significant and purposeful living. The great literature of all cultures, available in translation, and especially contemporary literature, he said, could more than supply the need for the man who was resolved to live in the modern age. Strauss denied that we can be Christian any longer in the traditional sense. While he drew a hard line between what he understood to be Christianity and modern thought, many today would say that the "old" faith can be nourished by the artistic expressions of the new age.

At one extreme are those who regard any work which satisfies the canons of artistic expression, possessing thereby its own integrity, as being essentially religious and, if honest, Christian. This position has been increasingly taken as the "subject matter" of such works is less and less derived from Biblical themes. Unlike the situation in the Middle Ages, drama today seldom has Biblical subject matter. Does this mean that there are no longer religious themes treated by dramatists? Hardly. But these themes are not obviously identifiable with Biblical materials. If they contain a "Christ figure," he will not be sinless, and his setting will be totally different from first-century Palestine.[13] For example, Samuel Terrien in reviewing the controversial play writes: *"Tiny Alice* extends further than the theater of the absurd, for it interprets mythical representations of self-will in the frame of a theology of allegiance to the ultimate. . . . It does not cheapen the price of living with the Presence."[14] This means that the religious life—understood as awareness of depth in all things —is nurtured not by a peculiar sort of art, a specifically "religious" art, but by all authentic artistic expression. But it also means that the religious life will not necessarily assume Christian forms unless "christology" is taken to be the truth of culture as a whole.

Another position is simply that artistic expressions are valid as descriptions or representations of the contemporary age to which Christians must address themselves. What is to be sought in literature, art, and music is not the Christian message, but the human problem—man in his misery and grandeur. Frequently cited as themes of contemporary expression are the "lostness" of the age, its complete relativity, its abandonment of metaphysical orientation, its repudiation of Christian standards. Modern expressions of culture keep us aware of the real world and man's desperate plight.

Others search literature for manifestations of specifically Christian themes: sin and alienation, judgment and reconciliation, the suffering of self-giving love, and so forth. Camus' *The Stranger* has been taken to represent the aimlessness of life cut loose from a God-reference; *The Fall,* the self-disintegrating results of refusal to assume personal responsibility; and *The Plague,* the ambiguous situation of modern man. Paintings such as Picasso's *Guernica* reflect man's destructive fragmentation and self-annihilation but also his refusal to surrender abjectly to demonic forces.

Why should Christians concern themselves with these expressions of contemporary culture instead of reading traditional devotional materials? The most important answer is that Christianity involves life in its wholeness rather than a single segment of it. The realities that theology recounts are not confined to a religious segment of life but constitute the truth of all life. Further, many people today simply cannot become interested in the classics of the past unless they have already reached a certain degree of theological sophistication. Finally, many of the classics advocate an approach to the Christian life which is repudiated today as fundamentally unchristian. The negative self-emptying of Thomas à Kempis' *Imitation of Christ* is one example. Although Luther published several editions of the *Theologia Germanica,* he later repudiated its influence. Calvin warned his followers that its spirit was different from the gospel.

People today must catch their devotions "on the run." Comparing the daily regimen of some of the "fathers" a century or more ago with our own situation will show the difference. They might rise at five, spend an hour at prayer, eat breakfast with the family, and devote thirty minutes to household devotions before beginning the work of the day. With the passing of the age of domestic servants, the relative leisure that schedule demanded has gone. Now there are the family tasks to share before a rushed departure to school and work. Frequently the mother is employed outside the home. If the father does not spend an hour or two a day commuting, the children may spend as much on a school bus. After work, the routine is much the same. Many families find it difficult to arrange even one meal a day together. What devotional reading is done must be caught on the run—five minutes with the family, short sentence prayers, perhaps some serious reading while commuting or before sleep at the end of the day, a sentence of Scripture propped up above the sink for the busy housewife to glance at during the day.

But if the Christian is to be able to use this material drawn from the whole of life, he must have guidance. Frequently a book which Christian leaders hail as pivotal is judged to be only dirty by church members. On the other hand, a steady diet of what he thinks is religious does not challenge the Christian to grow. At one time such guidance was exerted by the family. Protestantism laid great emphasis on the family and is at a loss to understand and cope with its decreasing significance today. The New Testament is not so committed to it as a scanning of Jesus' sayings will indicate. In lieu of family religion of an earlier period, many today are discovering the importance of small groups in the stimulation of Christian development. "We stir up one another to the new life in Christ by meeting together and encouraging one another," writes Robert A. Raines in the widely studied book, *New Life in the Church*. "A small group is necessary for this kind of personal and mutual encouragement."[15] It is this closeness of mutual concern which is the manifestation of what the New Testament calls *koinonia*, but *koinonia* cannot be known firsthand among hundreds of people. Reuel Howe in both his writings and his work with groups has stressed that in the mutual criticism and helpfulness of the group, we are saved from enmity toward each other.[16]

Recognition of the significance of small groups is not new. House churches are mentioned in the New Testament. Puritans and Pietists formed religious societies. The class meetings were one of the most important instruments of the Methodist movement. Bishop Robinson observes that the tendency has been to regard such groups as a technique for realizing some other end such as a more lively parish which is taken as the "real" form of the church. On the contrary he insists it is not a temporary expedient but a necessary part of the life of the body of Christ and must have the marks of true catholicity including celebration of the Eucharist.[17] In relation to the small group, the parish communion then manifests the wider unity created by Christ and limits the tendency toward the interest-group mentality.

The group is formed of five to twelve persons who pledge themselves to maintain certain disciplines. These may consist only of a common hour daily for mutual intercessory prayer or they may involve a more extensive plan for the use of time, money, and personal resources. A particular group can begin in various ways—a few people who are not satisfied with the quality of their Christian life and want to explore discipleship together, a study group that finds itself moving beyond intellectual discussion of ideas, a prayer circle that wants to break through the bonds of self-centeredness. Members agree to meet together twice a month or weekly for study, discussion, and prayer. They develop and revise their own disciplines which each member is expected to observe. Robert Raines's list is typical: weekly corporate worship, daily prayer,

Bible study, and giving of money, service, and witness.[18] Often the group will adopt a common project over and above its continuing study—tutoring school dropouts, supporting a preschool nursery in an area of need, looking after elderly or disabled members of the church. Involvement can be both personal and financial. Sometimes a limit will be placed on the period that the group remains intact to avoid cliquishness. Often persons outside a congregation will be enlisted through business or neighborhood association.

In the past a discussion of the Christian life has usually set out the stages of progressive development beginning in a heedless bondage to sin and moving through conviction, conversion, repentance, faith, new birth, and sanctification to possible glorification. It is more evident today that these are not so much chronological steps as theological abstractions and that Christian life is lived in the tension between the "law of God" and another "law in the members" but still in thanks to God (Rom. 7:22–25). A wider knowledge of both psychology and other religious traditions has raised doubts that such a progression of stages is definitely Christian in itself anyway.[19] Today the psychology of personality development is more likely to be in the background of any understanding of the Christian life.

The relatively new discipline of pastoral counseling has developed from the conviction that the psychological phenomena of religious experience cannot only be more accurately discussed in scientific terminology but that the whole complex of personal dynamics can be more certainly handled on the basis of knowledge derived from psychological research. To put it simply, psychologically oriented pastoral counseling stands to the ancient art of "cure of souls" as chemistry stands to alchemy. This does not mean that religion is an illusion from which men are to be weaned. But it does mean that scientific methods are used to obtain more reliable knowledge and develop more reliable methods of counseling.[20] This is part of the wider movement of desacralization that characterizes our culture. Paul Tillich has tried to use terminology derived from depth psychology to speak of the religious reality.[21]

Some have feared that this is only a substitute for Christian faith and have deplored the decreasing emphasis on sin, conversion, and willpower.[22] What is its significance for the Christian life? In the first place it means an enlightened application of concerned love which seeks full life for all men. Just as love manifests itself in providing food for the hungry and medical attention for the physically ill, so also it means trying to heal the wounds of emotional disturbance. In the second place it has helped to uncover the strategies by which sin is made to appear virtuous, and personal defects are disguised rather than remedied. In the third place, it has brought an understanding of human personality to the total ministry of the church. For example, expectations of the educational program can be coordinated with actual human capacities at various age levels. The picture of the mature Christian has been freed of aberrant overtones. Occasionally a new tyranny of the "normal" has been thrust on Christian life. But for the most part pastoral counseling has not tried to override Scripture or tradition but to help the pastor see that they find wholesome expression in life.

PRAYER

"The reason why prayer is difficult for many men today is that its traditional language leads them to imagine something which contradicts their empirical attitudes," writes Paul van Buren.[23] Since the days of Newton at least, any expectation of influencing the course of things by invoking supernatural intervention in this world has contradicted empirical attitudes. But if the bifurcation between nature and supernature is not acceptable science or metaphysics, neither is it sound Biblical thought. The Bible does not know such a bilevel reality: the regularities of life are no less the conscious will of God than are the remarkable events. Schleiermacher, influenced by both Reformed doctrine and Enlightenment thought, held that to suggest God change his mind and thus change the course of events was blasphemous: God's perfection is from eternity!

The implication is obvious: prayer can change nothing in the course of things. For most, the way out of the metaphysical and theological impasse has been to change the locus of God's activity from the world to the inner life— the spirit, mind, or heart. But the inner life too became the province of scientific probing and explanation, and the psychoanalysts claimed to have explained the origin of the religious illusion. Although there is place in their picture of a sane life for meditation and contemplation, the language of "Our Father" and "In Jesus' name" certainly suggests a different picture than such psychological dynamics would suggest.

Yet at the same time that theologians are trying to press home the full implications of the scientific world view, prayer cults have become more popular and books on prayer techniques continue to be written and read. A new interest in "speaking in tongues" has invaded even the more respectable denominations. While much can be said about its problematic nature for church administrators, for many it has meant personal experience shattering the expected boundaries of the possible. People describe it in various ways: "Fire!" "Ocean of liquid love." "Power of the Holy Spirit." "Something outside me." Rather than argue about it, many have spoken of it as a sense of a tremendous and hitherto unknown resource of power which has not only enriched their devotional life but has reinforced their service and witness.[24]

In his appropriation of Whitehead's philosophy for theological purposes, John B. Cobb, Jr., has tried to build a new metaphysical foundation for prayer. God is so constant in our experience, he says, that usually we are not only unaware of him but we can account for things without referring to him. Yet as different facets of experience can come to our attention—as when we are now more aware of external stimuli, now of our inner feelings—it is possible that God enters our consciousness in a unique sense. And when there is awareness of God along with our own persons, the experience is that of communion. Such an experience colors all experience and shapes one's interpretation of life. Its ontic reality demands some ontological accounting, and the immediacy of this interpretation makes it preferable to the roundabout psychoanalytic explanations frequently offered.[25]

The quasi-magical enlistment of supernatural resources has never been the aim of profound religion. Jesus said that God knows what we need before we ask him, therefore we pray, "Our Father. . . ." William Hamilton, while advocating a "radical" theology, admits in his *The New Essence of Christianity* that one is not likely to remain Christian without prayer. If nothing else, prayer means "space" for silence, waiting, and withdrawal. "So little is said today about private prayer in our kind of culture that makes real sense, and I do not wish to add to the empty invitations to pray that one finds on every hand."[26]

In his "theological experiment," Paul van Buren suggested that prayer's real meaning may be a concern for others coupled with thought about practical ways to help them. Thus prayer requires no supernatural reference at all.[27] Certainly many corporate prayers bear out van Buren's suggestion: their appeal does not reach beyond the immediate hearers. "Teach us that . . ." is frequently the minister's final word of instruction. Prayers of intercession concentrate on the possibilities of service which those actually praying might render: "Help us to feel compassionate toward others, to do all in our power to serve them. . . ." Many private prayers are little more than the attempts to conjure attitudes or feelings that one thinks he should have.

But discussion within these dimensions misses prayer's Christian meaning because that meaning does not grow out of some primitive metaphysic but out of faith; and not faith as blind attachment to a metaphysic reason cannot support, but faith in Jesus Christ. Calvin said that prayer is not natural to us: we must be taught by Jesus Christ and we pray through him. Luther said that the only true prayer is Christian prayer. Bonhoeffer warned about using prayer to "lay on a very nice show" for ourselves or of trying to listen to our own prayers in order to provide our own answers.[28] We can protect ourselves from ourselves only "by letting Christ alone reign in our hearts, by surrendering our wills completely to him, by living in fellowship with Jesus and by following him."[29]

This means that prayer is not a tool, not a technique for the Christian, but another aspect of the reality of faith: "Your Father knows . . . pray then" (Matt. 6:8–9). "What man of you, if his son asks him for bread, will give him a stone?" (Matt. 7:9.) "Fear not, little flock, for it is your Father's good pleasure to give you the kingdom." (Luke

12:32.) "He told them a parable, to the effect that they ought always to pray and not lose heart. . . . Nevertheless, when the Son of man comes, will he find faith on earth?" (Luke 18:1, 8.) It is not that Christians have extramundane resources available to them through faith but that Christian prayer is the life of faith. Or as Karl Barth has put it, "To be a Christian and to pray mean the same thing."[30]

Christian concern for others goes beyond the range of human power. What he most wants for others—as well as himself—is what no technique of his own can effect. This drives the Christian to intercession. As Lincoln once put it, "I went to my knees because I knew nowhere else to go." Yet just as the Scriptures admonish, "Seek, ask, knock," so there is a relationship between responsible action and God's "answer." God is not fate! While prayer does not answer problems in the direct empirical sense, problems can make one aware of dependence beyond superficial deficiency. Bonhoeffer could write: "While the bombs are falling all round the building, I cannot help thinking of the divine judgment, of the outstretched arm of his wrath . . . and of my own unpreparedness. . . . But when all's said and done, it is true that it needs trouble to drive up to prayer, though every time I feel it is something to be ashamed of."[31] Earlier he had written, "I am praying now quite simply for my release."[32] The absence of religion instead of ruling out prayer gives it fresh significance by freeing it from a province of life.[33] God is not found at life's borders where human powers play out.[34]

"Faith has to do with God," writes Gerhard Ebeling, "but one cannot speak about God unless he attributes to him the power above all powers." This power is not physical might nor human strength of will. "He therefore who knows the omnipotence of God in the cross of Jesus has learned what omnipotence means, and has learned it there alone."[35] The powerlessness of man for which faith is the answer is not human limitation in its usual sense but is manifest even in expressions of strength. That the sinner should be set free from himself—there is the power of faith!

Such a perspective on prayer should give much more freedom in dealing with the contemporary fact of dogmatic empiricism which could conceivably investigate and acknowledge "spiritual" influences of man over nature and other men. But that would not be a confirmation of Christian prayer. Although prayer is not a manipulation of the causal order of nature, it is the power which overcomes the world. (I John 5:4.) Robinson stresses that prayer must not be regarded as disengagement, something alongside activity in the world: it is rather penetration through the world to God.[36]

DISCIPLESHIP AND SUFFERING

"He therefore who knows the omnipotence of God in the cross of Jesus has learned what omnipotence means, and has learned it there alone."[37] There was a time when a romanticized concern to imitate Christ joined with a "spiritual" contempt for the body made suffering a definitive mark of the Christian life. Hair shirts, nail-studded belts, heavy chains, scanty food, and even flagellation were self-imposed techniques of identification with the suffering of Christ. Replacing that bizarre form of discipleship and in reaction to it was belief in the ongoing success of the historical process. Suffering was thought now to be contingent, not necessary, and preoccupation with it was regarded as morbidity requiring psychotherapy. In one seminary chapel the stained-glass windows portraying the ministry of Christ have no scenes from the passion. The victorious Christ invites men: come, learn, go—with no suggestion of the reality of the cross.

But the theme of this generation is different. "When Christ calls a man," wrote Bonhoeffer in the frequently quoted words, "he bids him come and die."[38] The words are the more poignant because of the underlining he gave them with his own life and death. Today the suffering attached to discipleship is not a pose to be struck. He called that a "pious but godless ambition."[39] Suffering is the inevitable result of obeying Christ in a sinful world. The necessity of suffering is not such that we must create forms of it for ourselves if our lives happen to be set in pleasant places. Its necessity is in the fact that the kingdoms of this world are not yet "the kingdom of our Lord and of his Christ" (Rev. 11:15). The cross is not something to contemplate: it is a reality of Christian witness.

The art of the church through the ages offers a running account of how it understood the meaning of being Christian. In the days of the Constantinian empire, Christ was portrayed as the Pantocrator in huge mosaics on the ceiling of the apse of the churches. He was the judge who held the power of the whole earth in his hand, the triumphant, commanding Christ—cold, stern, immobile. But as the power of the empire waned, the representations of Christ not only became more human, but suffering more and more characterized them. Christ on the cross rather than on the throne was the principal representation. And from the robed and crowned figure on the cross, the familiar crucifix portraying real human agony evolved. About the time of World War I the representations lost their divine aura to become simply that of a broken, suffering man. It is no longer even the divine Son of Man of Matthias Grünewald, but the man among men; and the horror of suffering is not the uncanny repulsion of killing the Son of God but the terrible horror of the daily experience of agony and death.

Much in the New Testament supports such an interpretation as against the early and perennial presupposition that the eschaton has arrived, making the suffering Christ a figure of the past. The epistle to the Hebrews speaks of Christ dying "outside the camp" of safety and respectability and calls men to bear abuse for him. (Heb. 13:12–14.) First Peter as a whole deals with the problem of Christians having to suffer—not for doing wrong which would be shameful, but in their Christian obedience. (I Peter 3:14; 4:1.) Paul speaks of making up in his own body what was lacking in the sufferings of Christ! (Col. 1:24.) Jesus had warned that his disciples were to expect persecutions. (Matt. 10:16–25.)

In *The Cost of Discipleship*, Bonhoeffer emphasized the positive place of suffering in the Christian community. He wrote of it as the transcendence over the law: "Under the law there is nothing that a man can suffer for his own *good*, still less for the good of another, and least of all for the good of Christ."[40] In the perspective of the law, suffering is the result of disobedience. In its Christian perspective, suffering means spontaneity and freedom. Christ has left a residue of suffering in his body, the church, which benefits that body—one man suffering for another. "Such vicarious activity and possibility on the part of the members of the Body is the very life of Christ, who wills to be formed in his members."[41] In writing about the "suffering of the messengers," he said that whereas the criminal suffers punishment in secret, disciples must stand before governors and kings so that suffering is part of their testimony.[42]

In *Letters and Papers from Prison* he wrote of the isolation of the sufferer who must stand against human commands—alone and in ignominy rather than as a public hero.[43] But later he said that his own sufferings should not be dramatized, that real suffering includes physical pain, and that there is a difference between the sufferings of the church and the "untoward experiences of her servants."[44] Whereas the religious man expects God to deliver him from suffering, Christ challenges man "to participate in the sufferings of God at the hands of a godless world."[45]

It would be easy in view of the contemporary cultural preoccupation with suffering and death to see this Christian emphasis in terms of the Promethean theme of hopeless endurance. William Stringfellow notes the perpetual temptation of Christians to make the gospel end with Palm Sunday in order to avoid the troubles and unsettling questions of the passion.[46] Yet neither does the gospel end with Good Friday. The Christ who calls disciples to suffer is the triumphant Christ who stands on the other side of death, whose victory has been won, and the sufferers are enrolled in that victory. Thus the agony of the world does have meaning beyond breeding imitators of Prometheus. Out of suffering comes justice when suffering has come out of love. Not blighted idealism but realistic discipleship is the emphasis. Not, "Let us also go, that we may die with him" (John 11:16), but, "In the world you have tribulation; but be of good cheer, I have overcome the world" (John 16:33).

Kazoh Kitamori's *Theology of the Pain of God* is built around the theme of God's "pain" in which Christians are called to share. God's immediate love for the world becomes wrath when it confronts man's rejection and sin, he says. God's pain is his resolve to love the world in spite of its sin. Such pain, however, is no obvious dimension of the world order itself: it must be revealed, even though men in various cultures have groped after its truth. In Jesus is the revelation of God's pain: he is God's pain.[47] Human pain derives from human sinfulness, but transfigured by the pain of God it can *serve* God's pain; that is, it becomes a witness.[48] Although the pain of God can best be understood in an age of pain such as ours,[49] it can only be understood in faith. In conclusion Kitamori returns to the note from Hebrews that Jesus suffers "outside the camp." If the gospel enters the city—that is, becomes an immanent dimension of this world—it ceases to be the gospel.[50] The theology of God's pain can never be dominant. It calls men to suffer.

There is danger that the contemporary theological emphasis on pain will be seen superficially as another sign of the end of the Constantinian era. For much of its history, the church has occupied a favored position in the West. Governments have catered to it. Its personnel have expected preferential treatment, which in our time has taken the form of clergy discounts in stores, hotels, and ticket offices or in the unique canons of publicity for "men of the cloth." The acknowledged stance of the *religious* conscientious objector (originally from the historic peace churches) only today is being met with a recognition of the stance of the nonreligious conscientious objector. There is frequently the implication voiced that the arrest and trial of clergymen (especially if they are prominent) as a result of public demonstrations is more heinous than such treatment of ordinary persons. It is in this light that Bonhoeffer's distinction between the suffering of the church and the suffering of individuals must be made. That Christians, lay and ministerial, have to take their place with everyone else in the world, subject to the same treatment, is not the fulfillment of the mission of suffering.

Nor is suffering an expedient form of public relations. "The blood of the martyrs is the seed of the church," has frequently been quoted with the implication that nothing would be better for the welfare of the church than a little persecution! People frequently side with the underdog, and if the church can identify itself in this role, it will lose the hostility of those who resent its prestige or are indifferent to its presence, some say. This may be true, but it is not the point of the call to suffer as disciples.

The call to suffer is the call to participate in the ministry of reconciliation. The Bible distinguishes between the world that belongs to Christ and the age that is under the control of the evil one. The evil forces have been defeated, the gospel announces, and Christians are enrolled in a "mopping-up operation" with its own dangers. The principalities and powers have been defeated. "What is meant," writes Cox, "is that these forces do not have the power to determine men. Rather, man has the power and the responsibility to rule over them and use them in responsibility before God."[51] Outside Christ's victory, these powers dominate man and dehumanize him by making him a pawn of fate rather than a responsible creature. These forces in contemporary society demean human life, whether in the inner city, the pockets of poverty, the organization of the church, higher education, industry, government, or the world of finance. And it is at these points as responsible laymen that Christians are called to obey Christ. Suffering is not the counterpart to commitment to a hopeless cause: it is the price of helping the world face up to the reality of the new age of Christ's victory.

What, then, does this specifically mean? In the first place,

it means whatever suffering goes along with an active concern for the world as against indifference, whether that is
due to hardness of heart or sheer ignorance. Second, it
means those practical steps of involvement which lead to
overcoming the disparity, with no illusion of the cost involved. Too much discipleship is good in short spurts but
lacks staying power. It takes its goal to be irrelevantly
idealistic as soon as it confronts the "facts of life." The
reality of suffering in connection with discipleship means
that this disparity is normal so far as the present age is
concerned and that therefore the disciple must bear it. He
neither has all the answers nor does he expect the world
to adopt enthusiastically the answers that he does have.
Kathleen Bliss warns that "Christians may fall into the
temptation of sharing the exaggerated moral aspirations
of a secular society which has replaced humble faith by
arrogant belief in its own large possibilities of doing
good."[52] Many have emphasized the stance of humility, of
"waiting on God"—but as Bishop Robinson suggests, "like
Nehemiah with a trowel in one hand and a sword in the
other."[53]

Chapter VI

Eschatology and Ethics

Against all the invitations to self-indulgence—"you owe it to yourself"—the Christian is called to discipleship. But because the obedience called for is beyond what the law requires and sometimes in the face of what statutes and traditions demand, the meaning of discipleship in the specific situations of daily life is often a racking question.

The Ethics of Discipleship

The current discussions of Christian ethics center on "contextualism" or "situationalism" which means that each situation requires a fresh, responsible decision as to what is to be done in it. Developing from the neo-orthodox emphasis on God's confrontation of man in the crisis of decision, contextualism builds on the work of Brunner and Barth and especially Reinhold Niebuhr[1] and H. Richard Niebuhr[2] of America. The pragmatism of William James provides the general orientation.

The fundamental concern of the contextualist is not simply a smooth-running social order but the development of human *persons*. If one can retreat from personal responsibility to immutable laws or established customs, he can avoid making his own decisions and hence the full dimension of being a person. By demanding conformity to law or custom, one stifles the growth of genuine persons. Therefore each individual is to be urged to make his own moral decisions in the light of man's collective experience but not in surrender to imposed schemes of behavior. Since the whole point of Christian ethics is the manifestation of the new man, the responsible man, it must manifest freedom in the context of God's love. In other words, Christians are not molded by a set pattern but are free to be the new creation in Christ with an integrity of heart and act.

Joseph Fletcher, who presents this approach, contrasts situationalism with legalism on the one hand and antinomianism on the other. Legalism lays down not only guidelines but specific directions which are to be observed without question in all situations. Thus, when Immanuel Kant held that we are required to tell the truth, even the truth of the location of the intended victim to a would-be murderer, he was a legalist. Antinomianism holds that each situation is unique and each person a law to himself, so that general principles applying to a plurality of situations are impossible. Situationalism respects the principles and traditions of a given community but sets them aside in any particular case "if love seems better served by doing so."[3] Love is the only universal: specific acts are contingent upon their situations.

An example of what the contextualist is driving at is the often-told story of the German fishing-boat master in the last war. He was part of an underground movement smuggling Jews out of Germany. One night as he was about to put to sea with several escapees hidden below deck, the port inspector came on board to ask who was with him. He answered: "No one. The war has taken all my help."

The officer, satisfied, permitted him to sail—to keep a planned rendezvous with some Swedes who would receive the escaping Jews. Although all the master's moral training held that it was wrong to lie, in this case that law was subordinated to love in saving human life where it could. The fishing-boat captain was a contextualist.

Of course, the key point in this position is the meaning of love. Fletcher gives us six propositions about it. First, love alone is intrinsically good. It is the only universal, but only as something we *do,* not *have.* "If a lie is told unlovingly it is wrong, evil; if it is told in love it is good, right."[4] Second, nothing but love is the norm of Christian decision and as such it replaces the law. "We follow law, *if at all,* for love's sake; we do not follow love for law's sake."[5] Third, love and justice are the same—that is, love is responsible and deliberative, not merely impetuous. Fourth, love is not contingent on *liking* the neighbor whose good it wills. The opposite of love is not hate but indifference. One need not have a "feeling" even toward God.[6] Fifth, only the end justifies the means—by which Fletcher means that only love can justify means. Finally, the decision of love can only be made in the concrete situation because "we can't always guess the future."[7] In fact, it must always be made in reference to the present, i.e., the present loving act, rather than to the future. The Christian, says Fletcher, answers the universal questions: What? love; Why? God's sake; Who? his neighbors. "But only in and of the situation can he answer the other four questions: When? Where? Which? How? These are, as we have suggested, the *kairos* factors."[8] Instead of "Do right and let the chips fall where they may," the situationist insists that what is right depends upon how the chips fall.[9]

Although the love ethic is characteristic of the Christian

community, says Fletcher, it is not peculiar to Christians. There is no double standard of goodness: "What is special is that the Christian's love is a *responsive* love."[10] It offers not a different norm but a different motive. "No, what makes it different is a theological factor; the faith affirmation that God himself suffered for man's sake to reconcile the world in Christ."[11] Yet not even the gratitude is unique: it is Christ taking form in the decisions of love— an expression borrowed from Bonhoeffer.[12]

Paul Lehmann, of Union Theological Seminary, avoids the garish illustrations that stab the reader of Fletcher's book, but he also tries to set contextualism in a more substantial historical and theological context. "Love" in Fletcher's writing remains vague. Like Luther, he assumes that neighbor-love needs no spelling out because it is patterned on self-love in which all men are experts. Love, therefore, need not be informed from outside itself. Fletcher specifically rejects Reinhold Niebuhr's emphasis on the distorting effects of sin as against H. Richard Niebuhr's stress on the human ability to respond to God's love.[13] This part of the discussion picks up the issue of the Reformation debate on the third use of the law mentioned earlier.

Lehmann speaks rather of *koinonia ethics,* that is, ethics in the context of Christ's presence in the world in the believing and forgiving community. As against the Pharisees for whom God's will was simple and known, Jesus, he says, had constantly to seek it. "There is no formal principle of Christian behavior because Christian behavior cannot be generalized,"[14] and this because the will of God cannot be generalized. God is himself constantly at work in the world keeping human life human, and what humanization is must be learned from Christ. The church, the koinonia, is the "laboratory of maturity."[15]

In this sense, ethics has to do with the "politics of God," that is, with what God is doing in the world. "The complexity of the actual human situation, with which a *koinonia* ethic tries seriously to deal, is always compounded of an intricate network of circumstance and human interrelationships bracketed by the dynamics of God's political activity on the one hand and God's forgiveness on the other."[16] Irrelevance or expediency in Christian conduct is the result of overlooking or denying God's continuing activity. For the Christian, the question is not "What ought I to do?" which implies both a double reality and a striving toward a goal which may never be reached, but "What am I to do?" which is answered by an indicative rather than an imperative.[17] In other words, being a Christian is not merely a "striving toward," it is fundamentally a "living in the reality of." Or, as Bonhoeffer put it in the opening chapter of his *Ethics:* "The knowledge of good and evil seems to be the aim of all ethical reflection. The first task of Christian ethics is to invalidate this knowledge."[18] And again:

One cannot, therefore, prove what is the will of God simply from one's own resources, from one's own knowledge of good and evil; on the contrary, only that man can do this who has lost all knowledge of his own of good and evil and who therefore abandons any attempt to know the will of God by his own means, who lives already in the unity of the will of God because the will of God has already been accomplished in him.[19]

One point the contextualists particularly stress is that the man who acts in love ought not to have a guilty conscience over violating some "absolute" standard. The fishing captain in our story ought not to feel guilty because he had to tell a lie in order to save the lives of several people. What he did was the loving and therefore the thoroughly right thing to do under the circumstances. John Wesley had a similar concern in his teaching about Christian perfection, and he ran into similar difficulty. Defining sin as a conscious violation of the known will of God, Wesley held perfection to mean the conscious intent of love in every decision and act. But over against this formal definition of sin is the material definition as anything contrary to God's will. To retain the integrity of the Christian life, he had to lay a countering emphasis on preaching the law so that discipleship would not be confused with blissful ignorance. What is there to keep a love ethic from foundering on human passion and self-deceit?

Douglas Sturm argues that as against these views that the divine imperative arises only from the crisis of decision a valid notion of natural law is possible "when a more adequate account is taken of the complete structure of the Christian understanding of reality"[20]—namely, God as creator, judge, and redeemer. Christ then is the same Word which is the law of man's creation and his significance is as wide as creation. "The appropriate form of human action is thus a repetition of the form of divine action. As God loves, so is man meant to love."[21] Presumably God's love is defined by the whole Biblical story. The aim is a mutualization of care and concern. The law is universal but its actualization is variable.

Does this approach to ethics imply a change of Christian conduct or only of its rationale? One of the favorite sources for illustrations has been sex, presumably because the discussion can tie itself to the change in moral standards since World War II. Statistics are readily at hand to document an increase in promiscuity, illegitimate births, and venereal disease among young people. The "supernaturalist" ethic categorically condemned sexual intercourse outside of marriage. The newer situation ethic speaks of the manifestation of love in the concrete situation: if this in a given occasion means extramarital intercourse, well and good. The situationist recognizes that any ethical decision must take into account ends, means, motives, and foreseeable results. If these are carefully evaluated, especially motives and foreseeable results, however, the decision made may not be so different from the answer that traditional ethics might have given.

Often the situationist does not make clear what range of experience he intends to bring to his decision. Thus, in discussing various circumstances under which abortion might be called for, Fletcher says that the situationists "would favor abortion for the sake of the [rape] victim's self-respect or reputation or happiness or simply on the ground that *no unwanted and unintended* baby should ever be born."[22] They would reason, he says, that there is no *human* life in an embryo in its early development. James F. Gustafson in reviewing the book asks: "Whose wants are considered? Is 'wanting' always the same thing? Many a mother on a day of misery during pregnancy wishes she were not having that child. Is that the day she decides for an abortion?"[23] To tell teen-agers that extramarital intercourse is permissible if love demands it is wrong, not because teen-agers lack integrity but because they lack experience. It is irresponsible to present a person with a choice when he has no basis for making a responsible decision.

Apart even from specific Christian commitment a wide enough range of experience might so shape the "foreseeable results" as to bring new appreciation for traditional thought, although it might also point to needed specific changes in attitudes. Only the rationale would have shifted

from "The Bible says" to "Human experience indicates"—
though the two might not be too different. At any rate, the
assumption that situationism necessarily means a "looser"
morality is not true, particularly when full responsibility
for a decision is stressed. If law does not absolve one of
responsibility, neither do attitudes unconsciously picked
up from the culture or subculture.

It is the significance of principle *within* love which Paul
Ramsey, the antagonist of the contextualists, stresses.[24] An
act is not wrong because it violates a rule as such, but
because it runs head against experience out of which the
rule has been developed. Each act is not absolutely unique,
or experience would have no value. Traditions require
fresh examination in view of fresh experience, but there
are valid guidelines which a Christian needs to keep in
mind along with his commitment to love.

The lie of the fishing-boat captain mentioned earlier
would have been completely ineffective for his purpose
apart from a rigid structure of truth. If the port inspector
had suspected that he was being answered in situational
terms, he would have searched the boat with disastrous results. The captain had to assume that in the vast majority
of cases the port inspector had been answered truthfully
so that he would not question this particular answer. Most
persons are familiar with the confusion and frustration
resulting from personal exchanges which are not grounded
on honesty but on what seems to be the loving thing to
say under the circumstances. In spite of the motive of the
person who shapes truth by his estimation of the feelings of
the other person, it is a serious violation of the freedom
of the one to whom it is done who should be able to make
his own decisions. A case in point is the question of whether
a person suffering from a terminal illness should be told

the truth about his condition. Psychologists are now saying that lying under these circumstances, even to spare the patient's feelings and possibly his life, creates a situation of distrust harder to bear than the truth of approaching death.

Another aspect of this question is the matter of using human beings for medical research. The science editor of *Saturday Review* has reported how Dr. Henry K. Beecher, of Harvard, has called attention to fifty experiments involving human subjects, in only two of which the patients were asked their permission. These studies had nothing to do with the patients' own immediate welfare. Although names and schools were omitted from the compilation as published in *The New England Journal of Medicine,*

> . . . there was no honest way to eliminate mention of the twenty-five young soldiers who acquired rheumatic fever because of an experiment they didn't know they were part of, or the twenty-three unwitting experimental subjects who died unnecessarily of typhoid fever, or the children whose thymus glands were removed by doctors who couldn't possibly have known the consequences of the surgery, or the deliberate and dangerous manipulation of brains and hearts and livers to satisfy other experimenters' curiosity, or the mother who died of metastasis of a cancer implanted in her body from the body of her dying daughter.[25]

Assuming that the doctors involved were not unscrupulous, they could have reasoned: love demands the experiments so that in the long run many more people might enjoy good health, and love further demands that I not worry these subjects with the possible dangerous results of the experiment when they may never materialize. Fletcher writes: "It becomes plain that as the love ethic searches seriously for a social policy it must form a coalition with utilitarianism. It takes over from Bentham and Mill the strategic principle of 'the greatest good of the greatest number.' "[26] The specter behind such talk is the Nazi regime with its brutal experiments on humans, not to mention the extermination of six million people. Indeed, as John Lear has indicated in an earlier article, certain American experimenters would be held guilty by the Nuremberg Code on the basis of which four Nazi doctors were tried and hanged—only the Nuremberg Code is not the law of the United States![27]

An intelligent ethical decision must be based not only on principle but also on knowledge. Love calls for the preservation of human life and the enhancement of human values. But *what* makes for the preservation of life is a matter of scientific knowledge or for scientific inquiry. Through such knowledge, the principle is fulfilled. Yet knowledge is gained only through experimentation, made possible as "irrational taboos" are dropped. Desacralization is the key not only to the modern world but to the fulfillment of the love ethic. Yet when are taboos irrational and when are they the expression of the value of human personality itself? When dare they be overridden and when must they be respected?

CHRISTIANS AND POLITICAL POWER

The ideal of Christian maturity is the coinciding of all one's inclinations and the demands of love. For such a person, no external law is necessary. To say the very least, however, not all men have reached that degree of maturity. And since at any one moment the world's population ranging from infancy to old age is scattered over the whole spectrum of maturing, no event in history can create a situation in which all mankind would enjoy the maturity envisioned by most contextualists. In the face of not only immature but also recalcitrant people, pressure must be

used to maintain an ordered society. In small societies public approval and disapproval may be sufficient to keep
order. In larger societies where relationships cannot be
personal, that approval and disapproval is expressed
through political structures. What use can the Christian
make of political power in the service of love?

A good share of the problem is the relation of the Christian as a citizen—possibly a magistrate—and the organized
church. There is a valid sense in which it can be said that
the church ought not to be involved in politics. The
church as a self-identified body of believers cannot become
a corporate political block although its members, dispersed
in the world, will participate in political structures. Ex-
ploring this matter, Paul Ramsey distinguishes the questions of *principle* to which the church as church must
speak "informing the consciences of men" and the specific
decisions implementing such principles which must be
made by those responsible for decisions on the basis of the
information they have available.[28] Ramsey believes that by
debating a plurality of specific decisions the church has
failed to address itself to crucial matters of policy. It ought
not to debate a specific instance of military intervention,
for example, for which it lacks the requisite evidence and
responsibility of decision, but the morality of intervention
in relation to its purpose. In the church's concern for the
Kingdom of God, writes Philippe Maury, "it is not within
the church's competence to define the means, legislative,
administrative, or educational, through which the necessary reforms should be achieved, and even less should it
describe the exact content of such measures."[29] He feels
that the organization of the ecumenical movement is useful
in gaining the worldwide counsel of Christians in formulating basic principles.

Any survey of church history would provide ample illustration of a point emphasized by Gibson Winter. When the church as an organization officially commits itself to a political program, it draws the lines of its fellowship in terms of that program. To enter the political arena is to be governed by the dynamics of politics. The church should help men to formulate basic guidelines but permit individual Christians the freedom to choose the implementation that seems best to them. Yet the church does have a role in encouraging people to assume political responsibility—which marks the difference between true community and a ghetto existence.[30] Paul Ricoeur makes a similar point in advocating "social action" in which the correctives of love can be exercised as against entering politics as such. The church gives light, he says, not through a power play but through its prophetic message.[31] One cannot maintain innocence but only limited guilt in politics. The purist is either a quietist or a terrorist—or, as Arthur Koestler put it in his book title, a yogi or a commissar.

Practically, this means abandonment of the perfection or nothing stance which has kept many active Christians out of politics except of the ecclesiastical sort. It means a much greater patience with the gradual approximation which the game of politics entails. It means a church that is free to discuss issues but also permits its laymen freedom to make the decisions for which they—and not the church —bear responsibility. It means that when extraordinary measures appear to be necessary, the broad experience of men given in principles will be accorded due weight in decision making. And it means that decisions honestly made will be entered into without backward glances in full awareness of the forgiveness of God and his sustaining purpose.

AND LIFE EVERLASTING

In spite of the continued use of a traditional theological vocabulary, contemporary thought centers in man—his life, his problems, his responsibility, his depth, and his frustration. The "theocentricity" of other schemes often turns out to be sheer gymnastics of words. The task of theology is not complete until it has expounded the meanings of doctrines for the lives of men. Whether this situation is as new as men once thought is another question. Perhaps the distinction between truth and illusion, between reality and representation has not been made *sub specie aeternitatis* but only in relation to an age. The illusion wasn't exploded: only the bothersome relation between two sets of symbols became evident.

At no point in theology does this situation have a better example than in the case with eschatology with which we must conclude. The "traditional" picture of a realm breaking in upon our world, judging it with ultimate standards, and rewarding it with unalloyed bliss or pain—all this sounds so contrary to what we can accept. But this has been the situation for a very long time. The preoccupation of the eighteenth century with immortality (Dr. Johnson could say this was the whole point of religion) was the frantic attempt to keep hold of the realm beyond. Since the Renaissance, man has increasingly sought to understand himself in terms of this world. Are the Last Judgment scenes then only of antiquarian interest or have they a counterpart in the reformulation of theology?

For Immanuel Kant the judgment is the condemnation of all our questionable maxims by the pure "Son of God," man totally obedient to the categorical imperative. The event is not outside man. It is man measured by his true self. Immortality is the infinite approximation to the goal of the Son of God. The Kingdom of God is the realization of the community of whole men, the true church emerging from ecclesiastical, historical faiths. Eschatology's reference, in other words, is here and now. It may speak of the beyond but it speaks to the present. It may refer to the beyond, but its relevance is the present.

Although Reinhold Niebuhr does not deny the fulfillment of history in a life beyond death, he holds that the pictures or images of "last things" are statements of faith about the whole meaning of history, statements which mold our obedience in the present.[32] Eschatological time is cumulative, which means that all meaning in history is caught up in it and therefore it is relevant to each moment. The Second Coming of Christ is not an event to be dated on the basis of cryptic references in Daniel and Revelation. It is an affirmation of the ultimacy of love. Love in this world is called to bear a cross. The victory of love then stands outside history. It is not a program to be reached by techniques. And love's victory in the exchange of the cross for a crown is not the cancellation of love which suffers here and now. Again, the resurrection of the dead means that all partial meanings are caught up in and not obliterated by the realization of God's purpose. Men are not expendable. Each one counts. Finally, the Last Judgment means that the measure of human accomplishment is not a human accomplishment. Nothing historical is ultimate, not even the structures of the church. Here we never have the last word. Christian eschatology's meaning is a limitation of the pretensions of the present life and a corrective of its aspirations. Niebuhr's exposition is typical of those who seek contemporary meaning in traditional forms. For many others the whole machinery of the "end" is only fantastic.

Paul Lehmann sets this discussion in the larger context of messianism to avoid the "far off" implications of a subject labeled "last things." This context more clearly rejects the temptation to speculate and to become irrelevant. The present reference furthermore avoids the dichotomy of present act and future result, as though love must have a reward beyond itself. Building on Barth's exposition of the "Second Adam," Lehmann insists that the new humanity is a present fact. "The difference between believers and unbelievers, both of whom are involved in the new humanity, is rather the difference between being in a situation which is hidden and being in one which is open."[33] The openness is not knowledge as against ignorance but confidence as against despair. The Second Adam keeps Christians from reverting from Christ to a "nature of man" unrelated to him. The power and glory of Christ's Second Coming mean the radical significance of Christ for history.[34]

In a somewhat different way Paul van Buren links eschatology to the present experience of the contagious freedom of Jesus. Through analysis of the language he notes that the kerygmatic message of the resurrection is not a description of appearances of the risen Jesus. "Risen" has an eschatological meaning. "The word 'risen' was at home in the context of such phrases as 'Kingdom of God' and 'a new heaven and a new earth,' which were used to point to the end and goal of all existence. The assertion 'Jesus is risen' takes the name of a historical man and says that he was of the realm of 'the end.' "[35] Verification of such a statement can only be in terms of whether the conduct of the one who makes it is consistent with it. Thus this statement of the ultimate significance of Jesus ("he was of the realm of 'the end' ") implies Jesus as the measure of true living. The eschatological has this present reference.

Rudolf Bultmann in his earlier work *Jesus and the Word* noted that Jesus refused to be a part of apocalytic speculation. The Kingdom of God, he wrote, did not interest Jesus as an ideal state, "but rather as a transcendent event, which signifies for man the ultimate Either-Or, which constrains him to decision."[36] "The one concern in this teaching was that man should conceive his immediate concrete situation as the decision to which he is constrained, and should decide in this moment for God and surrender his natural will."[37] In the later essay on "New Testament and Mythology," in which myth is identified as an expression of man's self-understanding, he links the cross and the resurrection as the eschatological event. This means for Bultmann that it has to do with faith which again has to do with understanding ourselves. Christians "participate" daily in the death and resurrection of Christ. In the preaching of the cross, the possibility of authentic life is opened to men.[38] Schubert Ogden, Bultmann's American disciple, says that the Christian confession is then: *"I henceforth understand myself no longer in terms of my past, but solely in terms of the future that is here and now disclosed to me as grace in my encounter with the church's proclamation."*[39] Bultmann distinguishes the theoretical possibility of new life which might be man's by information and the actuality which is not simply man's to command. Apart from Christ, man is dead and does not have in himself the possibility of authenticity.[40] Christ is the revelation of God's love that sets man free from himself to be himself through faith in that love: "The New Testament speaks and faith knows of an act of God through which man becomes capable of self-commitment, capable of faith and love, of his authentic life."[41] For Ogden, Christ is the decisive expression of the new reality that lies at the root of the Christian church.[42]

Except for Bultmann's existentialist appropriation of eschatology as the general category of faith, the views mentioned find a dynamic tension between the present and the yet-to-come which is significant for the present. "As it is, we do not yet see everything in subjection to him [man]. But we see Jesus . . ." (Heb. 2:8–9)—so the writer of Hebrews put it. The service of love in this world is not necessarily justified by a realistic view of the present situation, but it makes sense in terms of the Christian faith in the ultimate victory of love which is at the same time a goal in the struggle for clearer manifestations of love in the secular world. A hope which negates the significance of the present is not a Christian hope. In various ways it is emphatically stated that eschatology is not speculation but faith.

But there is another view, popular from time to time, which denies the tension between now and the yet-to-come. One example is Hegel's metaphysics where the perspective is always that of the end-time. This may be the result of seeing the world order in terms of an evolutionary development rather than from within the limits of a fall on the one hand and an eschatological fulfillment on the other. Present meaning has to do with the whole and is not derived from a yet-to-come. For Hegel, speculative philosophy plays the mediating role between man and God, not an age yet to come. The "new" age is already ours. Religious expression had reached its culmination in the incarnation—a present, not a past or future reality.

Today, Professor Thomas J. J. Altizer best exemplifies this point of view. For him, "the original heresy was the identification of the Church as the body of Christ"[43] because it set Christ over against humanity—a denial of true incarnation. To believe in the incarnation is to believe in Christ *manifest in the world*, not in the transcendent

Lord. For this reason Altizer rejoices in the "death of God" because it prevents the return (escape?) to transcendence. Nothing from the past can be the present epiphany. We must make a wager, he says: either the Christ of orthodoxy or Christ incarnate in the life of the world. "Dare we bet," he writes, "upon a totally incarnate Christ, whose contemporary presence negates his previous epiphanies, with the full realization that we are therein risking both the total loss of Christ as well as the loss of all that life and energy deriving from the presence of a transcendent and eternally given Christ?"[44] If we do, damnation and hell can no longer be excluded from our concern. Hell and guilt go together, however. Guilt is the result of repression, of retreat from life. Guilt is frozen in resentment which is surrender to pain. "A repressed humanity is a guilty humanity, whether it is conscious of its guilt or not, and to the extent that it becomes conscious of its guilt it must submit to the alien authority of the imperative, an authority sealing the finality of guilt, and binding humanity to perpetual repression."[45] To live in faith is to shatter the bondage of the law. To believe in a last judgment is to surrender Christianity to the law. Religious Christianity has reversed the incarnation. Freed from dread of an "alien beyond" we can participate in the present moment. But entailed here is the risk of moral chaos. The "death of God" proclaimed by modern prophets (Nietzsche is the model) reveals the chaos of meaninglessness to which we can react with the No-saying of slavery or the affirmation of the present moment, the opening of self to the "Christ who is fully present."[46]

But there is a dimension which neither the total focus of eschatology in the present nor its absorption into the present has dealt with. That is the unresolved tragedy of blighted lives. "All the children we worked with before leaving," reads a letter from friends away from their Haitian post eighteen months, "were dead on our return." One may be able to say yes to his own frustration, but can he say yes to the wards of mental patients, or yes to the dormitory inmates of a juvenal detention home or yes to the blank stare of war's victims? If he can, does the love of Christ have any meaning? True, the Christian is moved by the news of God's Kingdom to redress wrong and remove pain. But until the task shall have been completed, what then? Is there a dimension to Christ's love that reaches to those whom the world process has written off and forgotten? Not too much is said about this today. As William Hamilton says, today's mood is optimism. A hope in the final redress of wrong has too often displaced a live concern for present justice. Many retranslations of the gospel can handle that perversion, but whether they can deal with concern for the "least" without romantic confusion of feeling with reality is another matter.

Perhaps the New Jerusalem in which God's presence is no longer localized in a Temple is the counterpart to the reality of forgiveness in which we live. In spite of our love we leave ruins behind us and sometimes unresolved bitterness. We learn through Christ what it means to forgive, namely, to enter into the pain of God. But can we do this unless we know that forgiveness is not a palliative that enables us to endure a past we cannot change but that it is to participate in God's mystery of love in which the loose ends are tied and the empty places filled?

Notes

CHAPTER I. CHRISTIAN LIFE AS SANCTIFICATION

1. See Acts 15:1–21 and related passages.

2. John Locke, *The Reasonableness of Christianity*, ed. by I. T. Ramsey (London: Adam & Charles Black, 1958), Sec. 178, p. 45.

3. Augustine, "Eighth Homily on the First Epistle General of St. John," in *Augustine: Later Works*, tr. by John Burnaby (The Westminster Press, 1955), p. 322.

4. Søren Kierkegaard, *Concluding Unscientific Postscript*, tr. by David F. Swenson and Walter Lowrie (Princeton University Press, 1941), pp. 452 ff.

5. *Ibid.*, pp. 422–446.

5a. See Deane William Ferm, "Sex, Sin and Salvation in Sweden," *The Christian Century*, Vol. LXXXIII, No. 38 (Sept. 21, 1966), pp. 1142–1146, for a discussion of the contemporary situation.

6. Dietrich Bonhoeffer, *Ethics*, ed. by Eberhard Bethge, tr. by Neville Horton Smith (Macmillan Paperback, The Macmillan Company, 1965), pp. 60–63, 125–133.

7. Dietrich Bonhoeffer, *The Cost of Discipleship*, tr. by R. H. Fuller, rev. by Irmgard Booth (Macmillan Paperback, The Macmillan Company, 1963), pp. 45–47.

8. John Calvin, *The Epistles of Paul the Apostle to the Romans and to the Thessalonians*, tr. by Ross Mackenzie (Wm. B. Eerdmans Publishing Company, 1960), pp. 166 f. The commentary is on Rom. 8:13.

9. John Calvin, *Institutes of the Christian Religion*, ed. by John T. McNeill, tr. by Ford Lewis Battles (The Westminster Press, 1960), III.2.

10. Cf. Paul's, "I pommel my body and subdue it," I Cor. 9:24–27.

11. "An Excerpt of 'A Short View of the Differences between the Moravian Brethren (so called) and the Rev. Mr. John and Charles Wesley,'" *The Works of the Rev. John Wesley*, ed. by John Emory (J. Emory and B. Waugh, 1831), Vol. VI, pp. 22 ff.

12. John Wesley, "Letter to Conyers Middleton," *The Letters of the Rev. John Wesley, A.M.*, ed. by John Telford (London: The Epworth Press, Publishers, 1931), Vol. II, p. 380.

13. Carl Becker, *The Heavenly City of the Eighteenth-Century Philosophers* (Yale University Press, 1932).

14. Friedrich Schleiermacher, *The Christian Faith*, ed. by H. R. Mackintosh and J. S. Stewart (Edinburgh: T. & T. Clark, 1928), Sec. 5.

15. Karl Barth, *Church Dogmatics*, Vol. IV, Part 2, ed. by G. W. Bromiley and T. F. Torrance (Edinburgh: T. & T. Clark, 1958), p. 20.

16. *Ibid.*, p. 499.

17. *Ibid.*, p. 505.

18. *Ibid.*, p. 558.

19. *Ibid.*, p. 542

20. Paul Tillich, *Systematic Theology*, Vol. III (The University of Chicago Press, 1963), p. 46.

21. *Ibid.*, p. 420.

22. *Ibid.*, p. 422.

23. *Ibid.*, p. 149.

CHAPTER II. THE DEMAND FOR REINTERPRETATION

1. Bonhoeffer, *The Cost of Discipleship*, p. 69.

2. Dietrich Bonhoeffer, *Letters and Papers from Prison*, ed. by Eberhard Bethge, tr. by Reginald H. Fuller (Macmillan Paperback, The Macmillan Company, 1962), p. 162.

3. *Ibid.*, p. 163.

4. *Ibid.*, p. 167.

5. *Ibid.*, p. 195.

6. *Ibid.*, p. 196.

7. *Ibid.*, p. 197.

8. *Ibid.*, p. 200.

9. *Ibid.*, p. 201.

10. Mircea Eliade, *The Sacred and the Profane*, tr. by Willard R. Trask (Harcourt, Brace and World, Inc., 1959).

11. William Wordsworth, "Tintern Abbey," lines 94–95.

12. Friedrich Gogarten, *Demythologizing and History*, tr. by Neville Horton Smith (Charles Scribner's Sons, 1955), p. 87.

13. Schubert Ogden, *Christ Without Myth* (Harper & Brothers, 1961), pp. 25 ff.

14. Paul M. van Buren, *The Secular Meaning of the Gospel* (The Macmillan Company, 1963), p. 198.

15. William Hordern, *Speaking of God* (The Macmillan Company, 1964), p. 90.

16. John B. Cobb, Jr., *A Christian Natural Theology* (The Westminster Press, 1965), p. 15.

17. *Ibid.*

18. William Hamilton, *The New Essence of Christianity* (Association Press, 1961), pp. 55 f.

19. Joseph Fletcher, *Situation Ethics* (The Westminster Press, 1966), p. 108.

20. Barth, *Church Dogmatics*, Vol. IV, Part 2, pp. 25–27.

21. Søren Kierkegaard, *Philosophical Fragments* (Princeton University Press, 1936), p. 130.

22. Rudolf Bultmann, *Jesus and the Word*, tr. by Louise Pettibone Smith and Erminie Huntress Lantero (Charles Scribner's Sons, 1958), p. 8.

23. Bonhoeffer, "Single-minded Obedience," *The Cost of Discipleship*, Ch. 3.

24. Van Buren, *op. cit.*, pp. 188 f.

25. Gerhard Ebeling, *Das Wesen des christlichen Glaubens* (Tübingen: J. C. B. Mohr, 1959), pp. 17 f. E. T. by Ronald G. Smith, *The Nature of Faith* (Fortress Press, 1962).

26. Jean-Paul Sartre, *Existentialism*, tr. by Bernard Frechtman (Philosophical Library, 1947), pp. 26 f.

27. Gabriel Vahanian, *Wait Without Idols* (George Braziller, Inc., 1964).

CHAPTER III. THE WORLD COME OF AGE

1. Cornelis A. van Peursen, "Man and Reality—the History of Human Thought," *Student World*, Vol. LVI, No. 1 (First Quarter, 1963), pp. 13–21.

2. *Ibid.*, p. 16.

3. Harvey Cox, "The Gospel and Post-Literate Man," *The Christian Century*, Vol. LXXXI, No. 48 (Nov. 25, 1964), p. 1461.

4. *Ibid.*

5. Amedeo Molnar, "The History of the Faith," *Student World*, Vol. LVI, No. 1 (First Quarter, 1963), p. 42.

6. Harvey Cox, *The Secular City* (The Macmillan Company, 1965), p. 17.

7. Gabriel Vahanian, "Swallowed Up by Godlessness," *The Christian Century*, Vol. LXXXII, No. 49 (Dec. 8, 1965), p. 1507.

8. Cox, *The Secular City*, p. 36.

9. *Ibid.*, pp. 110–118.

10. *Ibid.*, Ch. 11.

11. Thomas J. J. Altizer, *The Gospel of Christian Atheism* (The Westminster Press, 1966), p. 102.

12. *Ibid.*, p. 103.

13. *Ibid.*, p. 112.

14. *Ibid.*, p. 107.

15. *Ibid.*, p. 146.

16. *Ibid.*, p. 156.

17. Arend Th. van Leeuwen, *Christianity in World History*, tr. by H. H. Hoskins (London: Edinburgh House Press, 1964), pp. 411–422.

18. William Hamilton, *The New Essence of Christianity*, p. 28.

19. *Ibid.*, p. 56.

20. *Ibid.*, p. 58.

21. *Ibid.*, p. 142.

22. *Ibid.*, p. 159.

23. William Hamilton, "The Shape of a Radical Theology," *The Christian Century*, Vol. LXXXII, No. 40 (Oct. 6, 1965), p. 1221.

24. William Hamilton, "The New Optimism—from Prufrock to Ringo," *Theology Today*, Vol. XXII, No. 4 (Jan., 1966), pp. 479–490.

25. Cox, *The Secular City*, p. 46.

26. Paul Tillich, *Systematic Theology*, Vol. I (The University of Chicago Press, 1951), pp. 8, 12–15.

27. See Bonhoeffer, *Ethics*, pp. 125, 137.

28. Karl Barth and Johannes Hamel, *How to Serve God in a Marxist Land* (Association Press, 1959).

29. Albert Rosenfeld, "A Laboratory Study of Sexual Behavior," *Life*, Vol. LX, No. 16 (April 22, 1966), p. 12.

30. Myron B. Bloy, Jr., "The Christian Function in a Technological Culture," *The Christian Century*, Vol. LXXXIII, No. 8 (Feb. 23, 1966), p. 233.

31. *Ibid.*, p. 234.

32. William Stringfellow, *Free in Obedience* (The Seabury Press, Inc., 1964), p. 26.

33. Gabriel Vahanian, *The Death of God* (George Braziller, Inc., 1961), pp. 182 f.

34. See Robert Lewis Shayon, "Historic Reversal for the FCC," *Saturday Review*, Vol. XLIX, No. 19 (May 7, 1966), p. 102.

CHAPTER IV.   THE LIVING BODY OF CHRIST

1. "By His power He is present in the sacraments, so that when a man baptizes it is really Christ Himself who baptizes," declares the Constitution on the Sacred Liturgy of Vatican II. *The Documents of Vatican II,* ed. by Walter M. Abbott, S. J., tr. and ed. by Very Rev. Msgr. Joseph Gallagher (Guild Press, America Press, Association Press, 1966), p. 141.

2. David Bakan, *Sigmund Freud and the Jewish Mystical Tradition* (D. Van Nostrand Company, Inc., 1958).

3. William Stringfellow, "Just So They Be There," *The Christian Century*, Vol. LXXX, No. 14 (April 3, 1963), pp. 431–432.

4. Stringfellow, *Free in Obedience*, p. 117.

5. *Ibid.,* p. 124.

6. John A. T. Robinson, *On Being the Church in the World* (London: SCM Press, Ltd., 1960), p. 97.

7. See, for example, Ronald C. D. Jasper, "Introduction," *The Renewal of Worship*, ed. by Ronald C. D. Jasper (The Oxford University Press, Inc., 1965).

8. John A. T. Robinson, *Liturgy Coming to Life* (The Westminster Press, 1964).

9. See Lester Kinsolving, "Demurrer on Jazzy Lord's Suppers," *The Christian Century*, Vol. LXXXIII, No. 25 (June 22, 1966), pp. 803–804.

10. See Bernard Anderson, *Rediscovering the Bible* (Association Press, 1951); Millar Burrows, *Outline of Biblical Theology* (The Westminster Press, 1946); A. M. Hunter, *Introducing New Testament Theology* (The Westminster Press, 1958); William Neil, *The Rediscovery of the Bible* (London: Hodder & Stoughton, Ltd., 1954); George E. Wright and Reginald H. Fuller, *The Book of the Acts of God* (Doubleday & Company, Inc., 1957).

11. See Robert McAfee Brown, *The Significance of the Church* (The Westminster Press, 1956); Daniel Jenkins, *The*

Strangeness of the Church (Doubleday & Company, Inc., 1955); T. Ralph Morton, *Community of Faith* (Association Press, 1954); J. Robert Nelson, *The Realm of Redemption* (London: The Epworth Press, Publishers, 1951); Lesslie Newbigin, *Household of God* (London: SCM Press, Ltd., 1953); Anders Nygren, *Christ and His Church,* tr. by Alan Carlsten (The Westminster Press, 1956).

12. Barth, *Church Dogmatics,* Vol. IV, Part 2, p. 620.

13. *Ibid.*

14. See George Huntston Williams, "The Role of the Laymen in the Ancient Churches," *A Symposium on the Laity* (Department of the Laity, World Council of Churches, 1958).

15. Hans Herman Walz, "Christendom in a Secularized World," *A Symposium on the Laity,* p. 57.

16. Bonhoeffer, *The Cost of Discipleship,* p. 266.

17. *Ibid.,* p. 269.

18. *Ibid.,* p. 271.

19. *Ibid.,* p. 297.

20. Paul L. Lehmann, *Ethics in a Christian Context* (Harper & Row, Publishers, Inc., 1963), p. 90.

21. *Ibid.,* p. 101.

22. *Ibid.,* pp. 112 ff.

23. *Ibid.,* p. 119.

24. Robert A. Raines, *New Life in the Church* (Harper & Brothers, 1961), p. 76.

25. Colin W. Williams, *Where in the World?* (National Council of the Churches of Christ in the U.S.A., 1963).

26. Hans-Ruedi Weber, *The Militant Ministry* (Fortress Press, 1963).

27. *Ibid.,* p. 65.

28. *Ibid.,* p. 93.

29. Hendrik Kraemer, *A Theology of the Laity* (The Westminster Press, 1958), p. 91.

30. *The New Delhi Report* (Association Press, 1962), p. 202.

31. Kathleen Bliss, *We the People* (London: SCM Press, Ltd., 1963), p. 76.

32. *Ibid.,* p. 109.

33. Daniel Jenkins, *Beyond Religion* (The Westminster Press, 1962), p. 82.

34. Walz, *loc. cit.,* p. 59.

35. Kathleen Bliss, "Introduction," *Signs of Renewal,* ed. by Hans-Ruedi Weber (Geneva: World Council of Churches, 1956), p. 5.

36. *Ibid.,* p. 6.

37. Eberhard Müller, "The Protestant Academies in Germany," *Signs of Renewal,* pp. 7–11.

38. T. Ralph Morton, "The Iona Community and the Training of the Laity in Scotland," *Signs of Renewal,* p. 24.

39. J. Edward Carothers, *Keepers of the Poor* (Board of Missions of The Methodist Church, 1966), pp. 84 f.

40. *Documents,* pp. 33 f.

41. *Ibid.,* p. 495.

42. Albert van den Heuvel, "Crisis in the Ecumenical Movement," *Christianity and Crisis,* Vol. XXVI, No. 5 (April 4, 1966), p. 61.

43. Bliss, *We the People,* pp. 97 f.

44. Walter S. Kilpatrick, "The Ecumenical Gap," *The Christian Century,* Vol. LXXXIII, No. 10 (March 9, 1966), p. 300.

CHAPTER V. PERSONAL LIFE IN THE BODY

1. Robinson, *On Being the Church in the World,* p. 93.

2. Rupert E. Davies, "Private Devotion," in Jasper, ed., *The Renewal of Worship,* p. 68.

3. William Hamilton, "The Shape of a Radical Theology," *loc. cit.,* p. 1221.

4. William Hamilton, *The New Essence of Christianity,* p. 86.

5. John J. Vincent, *Christ and Methodism* (Abingdon Press, 1965).

6. Kenneth Hamilton, *God Is Dead* (Wm. B. Eerdmans Publishing Company, 1966), p. 86.

7. Calvin, *Institutes,* I.6.1.

8. *Ibid.,* I.7.4.

9. Suzanne de Dietrich, *The Witnessing Community* (The Westminster Press, 1958); *The Word and His People* (The Seabury Press, Inc., 1958).

10. See Niels C. Nielsen, Jr., *God in Education* (Sheed & Ward, Inc., 1966). Philip C. Phenix argues that the area of concern should not be religious instruction as a separate discipline but rather making students aware of infinite depths and the presence of God in all life. See *Education and the Worship of God* (The Westminster Press, 1966).

11. Leonard Swidler, "Theology in the State University," *The Christian Century,* Vol. LXXXIII, No. 19 (May 11, 1966), p. 620.

12. Don Krasher Price, *The Scientific Estate* (Harvard University Press, 1965).

13. See, for example, Robert Detweiler, "Christ and the Christ Figure in American Fiction," in *New Theology No. 2*, ed. by Martin E. Marty and Dean G. Peerman (The Macmillan Company, 1965).

14. Samuel Terrien, "Albee's Alice," *Christianity and Crisis*, Vol. XXV, No. 11 (June 28, 1965), p. 143.

15. Raines, *op. cit.*, p. 78.

16. Reuel L. Howe, *The Miracle of Dialogue* (The Seabury Press, Inc., 1963).

17. Robinson, *On Being the Church in the World*, p. 84.

18. Raines, *op. cit.*, pp. 59 ff.

19. See John Baillie, *Baptism and Conversion* (Charles Scribner's Sons, 1963), especially in relation to William James's classic, *The Varieties of Religious Experience*.

20. See, for example, Anton T. Boisen, *Problems in Religion and Life* (Abingdon Press, 1946); Howard J. Clinebell, *Mental Health Through Christian Community* (Abingdon Press, 1965); Russell L. Dicks, *Principles and Practices of Pastoral Care* (Prentice-Hall, Inc., 1963); Edgar Draper, *Psychiatry and Pastoral Care* (Prentice-Hall, Inc., 1965); Seward Hiltner, *The Context of Pastoral Counseling* (Abingdon Press, 1961); Paul E. Johnson, *Psychology of Pastoral Care* (Abingdon Press, 1963); Wayne E. Oates, *Protestant Pastoral Counseling* (The Westminster Press, 1962); Carroll A. Wise, *The Meaning of Pastoral Care* (Harper & Row, Publishers, Inc., 1966).

21. See, for example, *Systematic Theology*, Vol. I, pp. 130 f., 288 f.; Vol. III, pp. 25–28, 281 f.

22. O. Hobart Mowrer, *Crisis in Psychiatry and Religion* (D. Van Nostrand Company, Inc., 1961).

23. Van Buren, *op. cit.*, p. 190.

24. See, for example, Morton T. Kelsey, *Tongue Speaking* (Doubleday & Company, Inc., 1964).

25. Cobb, *op. cit.*, pp. 227–235.

26. William Hamilton, *The New Essence of Christianity*, p. 128.

27. Van Buren, *op. cit.*, pp. 188 f.

28. Bonhoeffer, *The Cost of Discipleship*, p. 182.

29. *Ibid.*, p. 183.

30. Karl Barth, *Prayer and Preaching* (SCM Book Club, 1964), p. 19.

31. Bonhoeffer, *Letters and Papers from Prison*, pp. 127 f.

32. *Ibid.*, p. 87.

33. *Ibid.*, p. 164.

34. *Ibid.*, p. 166.
35. Ebeling, *op. cit.*, pp. 172 f.
36. John A. T. Robinson, *Honest to God* (The Westminster Press, 1963), pp. 91–99.
37. Ebeling, *op. cit.*, p. 173.
38. Bonhoeffer, *The Cost of Discipleship*, p. 99.
39. *Ibid.*, p. 190.
40. Bonhoeffer, *The Cost of Discipleship*, p. 273.
41. *Ibid.*, p. 274.
42. *Ibid.*, p. 238.
43. Bonhoeffer, *Letters and Papers from Prison*, p. 31.
44. *Ibid.*, p. 147.
45. *Ibid.*, p. 222.
46. Stringfellow, *Free in Obedience*, p. 35.
47. Kazoh Kitamori, *Theology of the Pain of God* (John Knox Press, 1965), p. 40.
48. *Ibid.*, p. 72.
49. *Ibid.*, p. 137.
50. *Ibid.*, p. 150. Cf. Gabriel Vahanian: "An immanentist Christian can only be a pseudo-Christian. He points in the same breath to his God and to his success" (*The Death of God*, p. 206).
51. Cox, *The Secular City*, p. 128.
52. Bliss, *We the People*, p. 118.
53. Robinson, *Honest to God*, p. 101.

Chapter VI. Eschatology and Ethics

1. Reinhold Niebuhr, *Moral Man and Immoral Society* (Charles Scribner's Sons, 1932).
2. H. Richard Niebuhr, *The Responsible Self* (Harper & Row, Publishers, Inc., 1963).
3. Fletcher, *op. cit.*, p. 26.
4. *Ibid.*, p. 65.
5. *Ibid.*, p. 70
6. *Ibid.*, p. 108.
7. *Ibid.*, p. 136.
8. *Ibid.*, p. 142.
9. *Ibid.*, p. 144.
10. *Ibid.*, p. 155.
11. *Ibid.*, p. 156.
12. Bonhoeffer, *Ethics*, p. 82.
13. Fletcher, *op. cit.*, pp. 151 f.

14. Lehmann, *Ethics in a Christian Context*, p. 77.
15. *Ibid.*, p. 101.
16. *Ibid.*, p. 141.
17. *Ibid.*, p. 131.
18. Bonhoeffer, *Ethics*, p. 17.
19. *Ibid.*, p. 39.
20. Douglas Sturm, "Naturalism, Historicism, and Christian Ethics," *New Theology No. 2.*, p. 85.
21. *Ibid.*, p. 89.
22. Fletcher, *op. cit.*, p. 39.
23. James F. Gustafson, "How Does Love Reign?" *The Christian Century*, Vol. LXXXIII, No. 20 (May 18, 1966), p. 655.
24. Paul Ramsey, *Deeds and Rules in Christian Ethics* (Edinburgh: Oliver & Boyd, Ltd., 1966).
25. John Lear, "Experiments on People—The Growing Debate," *Saturday Review*, Vol. XLIX, No. 27 (July 2, 1966), p. 43.
26. Fletcher, *op. cit.*, p. 95.
27. John Lear, "Do We Need New Rules for Experiments with People?" *Saturday Review*, Vol. XLIX, No. 6 (Feb. 5, 1966), p. 65.
28. Paul Ramsey, "The Church and the Magistrate," *Christianity and Crisis*, Vol. XXV, No. 11 (June 28, 1965), pp. 136–140.
29. Philippe Maury, *Politics and Evangelism*, tr. by Marguerite Wieser (Doubleday & Company, Inc., 1959), p. 72.
30. Gibson Winter, "The Churches and Community Organization," *Christianity and Crisis*, Vol. XXV, No. 9 (May 31, 1965), pp. 119–122.
31. P. Ricoeur, "Ye Are the Salt of the Earth," *A Symposium on the Laity*, pp. 39–50.
32. Reinhold Niebuhr, *The Nature and Destiny of Man* (Charles Scribner's Sons, 1943), Vol. II, Ch. 10, "The End of History."
33. Lehmann, *op. cit.*, p. 120.
34. *Ibid.*, p. 122.
35. Van Buren, *op. cit.*, p. 131.
36. Bultmann, *Jesus and the Word*, p. 41.
37. *Ibid.*, p. 131.
38. Rudolf Bultmann, "New Testament and Mythology," *Kerygma and Myth*, ed. by Hans Werner Bartsch, tr. by Reginald H. Fuller (Harper & Brothers, 1961), pp. 38–43.

39. Ogden, *op. cit.*, p. 114.
40. Bultmann, "New Testament and Mythology," *loc. cit.*, pp. 28 f.
41. *Ibid.*, p. 33.
42. Ogden, *op. cit.*, pp. 17 f.
43. Altizer, *op cit.*, p. 132.
44. *Ibid.*, p. 138.
45. *Ibid.*, p. 143.
46. *Ibid.*, p. 155.

Index

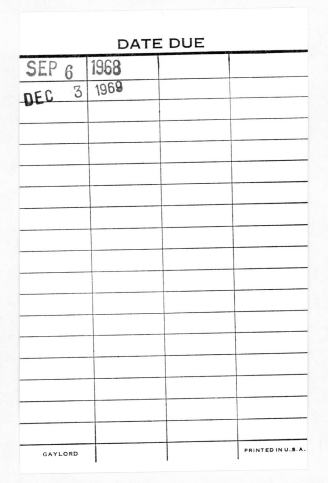

DATE DUE

SEP 6	1968		
DEC 3	1969		
GAYLORD			PRINTED IN U.S.A.